THE MEN WHO CHANGED THE COURSE OF HISTORY

Jesus, Napoleon, Moses, Julius Cesar, Saint Paul, Alexander the Great, Gandhi & Muhammad. Lessons from the Great Men that Forged our Society.

- SECOND EDITION -

By Dominique Atkinson

© **Copyright 2015**

All rights reserved. No part of this book may be reproduced or transmitted in any form or by any means, electronically or mechanically, including photocopy, recording, or by and information storage or retrieval system, without the written permission from the publisher, except in the case of brief quotations embodied in critical articles or reviews.

Trademarks are the property of their respective holders. When used, trademarks are for the benefit of the trademark owner only.

DISCLAIMER

The information provided herein is stated to be truthful and consistent, in that any liability, in terms of inattention or otherwise, by any usage or abusage of any policies, processes, or directions contained within is the solitary and utter responsibility of the recipient reader. Under no circumstances will any legal responsibility or blame be held against the publisher for any reparation, damages, or monetary loss due to the information herein, either directly or indirectly. Respective authors hold all rights not held by publisher.

Note from the Author:

Destiny is both unpredictable and fickle. Jesus, Napoleon, Moses, Julius Cesar, Saint Paul, Alexander the Great, Gandhi & Muhammad were men whose lives changed the course of history. They would have been remarkable in any era in which they were born. But by living when they did, each defined the times in which they lived. Their actions transformed the imprint of their countries and the world.

Caesar in the ancient world and Napoleon in the 19th century had different challenges, but both men faced them with energy, drive, and a hard-edged intuition. Jesus and Alexander lived approximately the same number of years, and each life span brought conquest in different forms, the former by winning souls from death on a cross, the latter from gaining land at the point of a spear. St. Paul and Constantine, separated by several centuries, both altered their landscapes in service to the same God. Moses and Gandhi, in vastly different ways, brought the power of law, justice and faith to the fore as they liberated their people. Although Muhammad was tutored by an angel and instructed by the holy, he never lost sight of his own humble human status.

Join me in learning about these great men! It's by studying their lives that we gain a sense, not only of who they were, but of what we have become as a civilization because of their influence. If any of these men were to be taken out of history's record, the ensuing gap would be enormous. As we study the past, we can look back on their achievements and be glad that we journey upon the roads that they paved for history to travel.

It's worthwhile to examine these remarkable men and the lives they lived. In doing so it's interesting to ask difficult questions. What would they be like if they lived today? How would Paul or Muhammad summon believers to follow a faith when it's not dangerous to be a believer? For Christians who believe that Jesus will return, will they recognize him in modern times? Could Alexander and Napoleon have confined their talents to administrative innovation rather than military conquest? Would Constantine and Caesar have been able rulers if they did not also have to lead armies? Would Gandhi, the most recent of the men studied in these chapters, approve of the way his country has evolved politically and spiritually? How would Moses look today if he were less majestic in his stature?

Would ordinary life suit the man who talked to God?

All of them raise questions about what it is to live a life so fully, for there can be no doubt that these men held nothing back. Not for them a half-hearted existence; they poured everything they had into their endeavors. Let's get to know them!

Chapter Index

Introduction 10

Chapter One: Moses the Lawgiver 13

    Who was Moses?...13

    In the Beginning..14

    Early Influences 16

    Moses' Life Changes 18

    The Israelites after Moses 25

    Why Moses Matters 27

Chapter Two: Alexander the Great 29

    Who was Alexander?..29

    In the Beginning..29

    Early Influences 30

    Alexander's Life Changes.......................................34

    Macedon after Alexander......................................41

    Why Alexander Matters 42

Chapter Three: Julius Caesar the Conqueror 45

    Who was Julius Caesar?..45

    In the Beginning..45

    Early Influences 46

    Caesar's Life Changes 48

    The Empire after Julius Caesar 54

    Why Caesar Matters 55

Chapter Four: Jesus the Christ 59

    Who was Jesus?..59

    In the Beginning...59

    Early Influences 61

    Jesus' Life Changes 62

    Christianity after Jesus..............................71

    Why Jesus Matters 72

Chapter Five: St. Paul the Evangelist 73

    Who was St. Paul?.....................................73

    In the Beginning...73

    Early Influences 75

    Paul's Life Changes 75

    Christianity after Paul 81

    Why Paul Matters......................................82

Chapter Six: Constantine the Great.................84

    Who was Constantine?..............................84

- In the Beginning...84
- Early Influences 86
- Constantine's Life Changes..................................86
- The Empire after Constantine 95
- Why Constantine Matters 95

Chapter Seven: Muhammad the Prophet 97
- Who was Muhammad? 97
- In the Beginning...97
- Early Influences 98
- Muhammad's Life Changes 100
- Islam after Muhammad......................................106
- Why Muhammad Matters 107

Chapter Eight: Napoleon the Emperor......................109
- Who Was Napoleon?..109
- In the Beginning...109
- Early Influences 111
- Napoleon's Life Changes 115
- France after Napoleon.......................................122
- Why Napoleon Matters 123

Chapter Nine: Gandhi the Mahatma........................125

Who was Gandhi?..125
Early Influences 125
Gandhi's Life Changes...128
India after Gandhi..135
Why Gandhi Matters 135
**** PREVIEW OTHER BOOKS BY THIS AUTHOR****
....137

Introduction

The 21st century stands witness to the achievements of some of the most influential men in the world. And yet, no matter how today's movers and shakers stand in contemporary rankings, how can we compare them to the giants of the past, the men who took history in their bare hands and bent it to their will? Whether they strode upon the stages of military power or at the altars of religious belief, they have left their marks on civilization.

Accustomed as we are to the rule of law, we risk forgetting that the legend of Moses the Lawgiver and his acquisition of the Ten Commandments is the landmark event in Jewish pre-history. Those original stone tablets have been the midwife to numerous judicial children, blending the obligations of moral law with the requirements of civil and criminal law in a succinct body.

Bill Gates and Microsoft transformed the way in which data could be collected and compiled; when Gates retired to leave his desktop empire behind in favor of philanthropy, was it because he was ready for a new phase in his life or was it because, as the legend says of Alexander the Great, there were no worlds left to conquer?

How would Constantine's predecessor, Julius Caesar, have reacted if he'd known that over 300 years after his reign, a subsequent emperor would turn his back on the Roman gods and embrace Christianity, a religion that began with the ministry of an obscure carpenter from an insignificant region of the empire and evolved into a faith practiced by billions? And, centuries later, how does the upstart Corsican Napoleon rank as the military leader who created an empire with himself as its head, reminiscent of Caesar, and redesigned his nation?

How do the advances made by cell phone technology that have been so integral to the Apple empire founded by the late Steve Jobs compare to the letters, journeys, and missionary zeal of Saint Paul, who traveled with that obscure carpenter's story across thousands of miles, braving shipwrecks, pirates, prison, and ultimately, execution?

What was the force in the desert that stirred up the Prophet Mohammed and inspired the birth of a religion whose believers will make up more than an estimated 50 percent of the population in 50 countries?

The names of these men have echoed through the halls of history since their exploits reconfigured the maps, laws, beliefs, and annals of the past. Today we live in a world shaped by their footprints. But what do we know of these game-changers? Immersed as we are in social media, headlines, 24-hour news and the Internet, how can we effectively evaluate the parts that these men played when they occupied the stage of world events?

Chapter One: Moses the Lawgiver

Who was Moses?

Moses never went to law school. Nor did he have any prior experience as a tour guide. It's obvious that the man who led his travelers on a 40-year journey through the wilderness lacked a GPS; cynics might even say that he lacked any sense of direction. But Moses was not appointed by God to lead the people of Israel because of his navigational skills. He was charged not only with freeing an enslaved people but with forging them into a nation: 12 tribes with a primitive awareness of one deity, transformed into a people whose commitment to the law and to monotheism would give them the skills they would need to survive in a world that all too often proved hostile.

Moses stands tall in an ancient time when men and myth frequently merged, until the saga becomes embedded in truth, regardless of what can be proven. Archeologists, historians, and theologians cannot reach a consensus about the man who is revered by the three major monotheistic religions of Judaism, Christianity, and Islam. His life is estimated to have taken place as long ago as 1500 years before the birth of Jesus Christ, but a man of this stature bestows upon the millennia a sense of eternity because his legacy, the Ten Commandments, is as relevant now as when the tablets first appeared.

It's not as though there were no laws before Moses. After all, Hammurabi's Code established a legal system for the Babylonians approximately several centuries before Moses is estimated to have made his appearance. However, Hammurabi's legal doctrine was more of a civil structure than Moses' laws, which were based upon the moral code ordained by God. Viewed in another light, there are no Hollywood movies starring A-list actors telling the story of Hammurabi. *Exodus*, the story of Moses starring Christian Bale, was a Hollywood blockbuster. And before Bale, there was Charlton Heston taking on the role of the Hebrew leader in The Ten *Commandments*. But who is the character of Moses outside of today's silver screen and the Bible?

In the Beginning

Moses entered history in the Old Testament Book of Exodus at a time when his people, the Israelites, who went to Egypt generations before to escape a famine, had been downgraded from royal favorites to royal slaves. No one could have predicted that when the patriarch Jacob and his sons journeyed to Egypt where his favorite son, Joseph, had become the pharaoh's chief advisor, how quickly the tribe would become a cohesive people, and then a minority of the population. But as their numbers grew, and Joseph and his influence were gone, the foreign visitors who came to stay became intruders, with no royal presence to protect them. The Egyptian pharaoh, fearing that the fertility of the Israelites would overwhelm the population of his country, devised a ruthless solution. The midwives were ordered by the pharaoh to let infant girls live, but to kill the boys. The Bible says that the midwives obeyed God, and refused to kill the baby boys. Their response, when asked by the pharaoh why the Israelites continued to have male children, was that Hebrew women gave birth before the midwives arrived.

A modern saying asserts that behind every great man is a great woman. Moses' early life was a testimonial to these words because his very existence depended upon the courage of women: first the brave midwives who risked pharaoh's ire to protect the children they delivered, and then his mother Jochebed, who defied the decree. When her baby boy was born, the Book of Exodus tells us that she placed her son in a basket in the reeds on the banks of the Nile. When the pharaoh's daughter went to bathe in the river, she found the basket and adopted the baby, naming him Moses, an Egyptian and not a Hebrew name. Exodus relates that Moses' older sister Miriam, conveniently on site when the baby was discovered, offered to find an Israelite nurse for the baby. The royal infant's biological mother was the nurse; it's easy to see that Moses came from a most resourceful family, with female relatives who knew how to maneuver in a dangerous world. That resourcefulness would stand Moses in good stead in the years to come.

Early Influences

As a member of the royal household, Moses would have lived a life of privilege. We know nothing of those early years, although cinematic accounts have created scenes which, while entertaining, fail to fill in the gaps. However, he was aware of his own heritage, and knew that he was not an Egyptian by birth. But something must have summoned him back to his roots for him to be on the scene where the Israelites were working. Was Moses pulled between the call of his own heritage and the familiarity of his upbringing? The choices were stark: the life of a slave compared to the life of a prince. There's no way to know, and early

Biblical writing wasn't known for its psychological analysis. What we do know is that, one day, when Moses saw an Egyptian beating an Israelite, he lost his temper—Moses' temper would get the better of him more than once—and killed the Egyptian. His act was not appreciated by his people; when Moses tried to break up a fight between two Israelite slaves, one of the men challenged him by asking him if he intended to kill him as he had the Egyptian. The slaves likely knew that he was one of them by birth but he had escaped their fate. That he was three months old when the Egyptian princess claimed him, and in no position to have influenced her decision was irrelevant to the Hebrews. They lived in slavery, he did not.

Moses had not concealed his act as well as he thought. Some scholars believe that when Moses was an adult, the ruling pharaoh was Thutmose III, a brilliant military tactician with a history of ruthless actions. Moses apparently felt—correctly, as it turned out—that his quasi-royal status would not save him from the wrath of the pharaoh. With his life in danger from the pharaoh, Moses fled from Egypt and made his way to Midian in northwestern Arabia.

Moses began a new life in a new land. He had made a good impression by coming to the rescue of seven young women when shepherds tried to prevent them from watering their flocks of sheep. He was a foreigner to them; they told their father that their rescuer was an Egyptian. Moses married Zipporah, one of the seven, and began a family. But he clearly was aware that he was not among his own people, at a time when tribal bonds were part of an individual's identity. When his son is born, he names him Gershom, saying, "I have become a foreigner in a foreign land." When he lived in Egypt, he was seen as an Egyptian by the Hebrew people. The Midianites saw him as an Egyptian. But he needed to define himself.

His life must have seemed a far cry from his daily routine in Midian, but his destiny seemed to be decided; he was a husband, a father, a shepherd. But the situation in Egypt had not changed, even though he was no longer a part of it; although he was distant from the scene, the cruelty to the Israelites had only increased.

Moses' Life Changes

One day, while tending to his father-in-law's flocks, Moses had a visit from a being whose status surpassed anything at the Egyptian court. He saw a bush on fire, but he could tell that nothing was burning. Intrigued, Moses went closer. But not too close—a voice from the bush told him not to come nearer because he was on holy ground. And then came an introduction that was to change the course of history. "I am the God of your father, the God of Abraham, the God of Isaac, and the God of Jacob." Frightened, Moses hid his face.

God then proceeded to conduct one of the most unusual job interviews ever recorded. Moses, God said, was to go to Egypt and rescue the Israelite slaves so that he could bring them to freedom in a prosperous new land. Moses wanted to know, logically enough, why he was the one to do this task. God answered the question behind the question, telling Moses that God would be with him. But Moses was by no means easy to convince. He reminded God that God had been a stranger to the Israelites; they would need to be introduced. God provided the introductory information, but for someone who was searching for ID, God's credentials were lacking. How is he supposed to represent God to the Hebrews who are convinced that God has forgotten them when God says, "This is what you are to say to the Israelites: 'I am who I am. I am has sent me to you."

Moses proved his mettle by continuing to probe God. What if they didn't believe that Moses was sent by God? He reminded God that he wasn't eloquent

(Moses was said to stutter). Moses asked how he could convince the Israelites that he was sent by God to deliver them from the Egyptians.

Suddenly it was God who had to present his credentials. He transformed Moses' staff into a serpent and then back into a staff; he afflicted Moses' hand with leprosy and then healed it. But Moses didn't capitulate, another trait that would serve him well when he was facing an intransigent monarch in Egypt. Moses explained again that he wasn't a smooth talker; he would need help if he were to take on this mission. There is poignancy in his response when he tells God that he's not eloquent and hadn't become so since God opened the conversation. Finally, God agreed to allow Moses' older brother Aaron to accompany Moses on this mission. God had good news to impart. The people in Egypt who wished Moses ill are dead. It's safe for him to return.

Aaron was Moses' intermediary with the Israelites, convincing them that God intended to rescue them from bondage. But the pharaoh was not so obliging. From the beginning, he proved himself to be hard of heart, just as God had predicted. When Moses and Aaron ask for him to let the people go so that they can worship God in the wilderness, the pharaoh wants some ID, and perhaps a pedigree. His reply was arrogant, as he asked them who this god was. The pharaoh was sufficiently familiar with the gods of the Egyptian pantheon—Ra, Anubis, Isis, Osiris—to show his disdain for an unknown god. The Israelites would not be freed to worship their god, and the pharaoh punished them for the request. From now on, the overseers were not to provide straw for the slaves to use to make bricks. The Israelites would have to get the straw on their own. Moses' first foray into the rescue of his people proved a dismal failure.

But something happened to Moses, something transformational. He confronted God. "Ever since I went to Pharaoh, he has brought trouble on this people and you have not rescued your people at all." God gives his assurance that he has not forgotten the Israelites and in fact is acting on the promise he made to the patriarchs Abraham, Isaac, and Jacob.

But the pharaoh's heart is hardened. Stubbornly he refused to release his slaves, even though his land was cursed by a series of plagues, a succession of disasters that, if it happened in modern times, would have had television crews and reporters from every corner of the globe showing up to chronicle the events. The story of the plagues spread beyond Egypt; according to the book of I Samuel in the Bible, the Philistines even knew the story. First, the waters of Egypt turned to blood; the plague extended not only to the bodies of water but also to the water that was in wooden and stone vessels. The second plague brought frogs from the river to the homes, beds, ovens, kneading troughs, even the people of Egypt. Next, the dust of Egypt turned into gnats, followed by swarms of flies. The next plague struck the livestock with disease. Plague number six transformed the handfuls of ashes that Moses sprinkled toward the heavens in full view of the pharaoh; the ashes turned to dust, and became boils upon the people and the animals, throughout Egypt. Thunder and hail, unlike anything ever seen in Egypt, struck next. As the pharaoh continued to be intransigent, locusts covered the face of the earth, devouring every tree growing out of the field. The ninth plague brought darkness all over Egypt for three days. Pharaoh stubbornly remained unyielding; the Israelites could not go.

Until the last, terrible, inevitable plague. The tenth plague sent the Angel of Death to the households of the Egyptians but passed over the Israelite homes, an event commemorated in the symbolic holiday of Passover. Grieving at the death of his heir and the monumental loss of life, the pharaoh released the

Israelites from captivity and they began their journey from enslavement to freedom under Moses' leadership. But then the pharaoh changed his mind, called for his warriors and chariots, galloped off in pursuit of his escaping slaves, and nearly overtook them. Then Moses raised his staff, and the waters of the Red Sea parted, allowing the Israelites to cross on dry land. But when the Egyptians followed, the walls of water engulfed them and they drowned.

Life, however, would prove to be very different on the other side of the sea, as Moses became a full-time nanny to a people who had grown so accustomed to enslavement that, instead of rejoicing in their liberation, they berated their liberator because their meals no longer had the same seasonings and flavor as those they enjoyed in Egypt. For the sake of a good meal, it seemed, the Israelites were ready to relinquish their freedom.

Their complaints and accusations sorely tried Moses' patience. It became Moses' task to teach the former slaves that with freedom came responsibility, both to one another and to God. He went up to Mount Sinai to receive the stone tablets upon which were written the laws that God had decreed his people were to live by. He was up on Mount Sinai a long time, as God delivered to him not only the ten laws by which the Israelites were to live, but also a code by which a society would be formed. The Israelites were uneasy without the presence of their protector and rescuer, and they found themselves in need of a god. They wanted a god that they could see. Aaron obliged; he ordered them to bring their jewelry so that a god could be formed. The golden calf of their making became the focus of their worship.

God, seeing their actions, sent Moses back down from Mount Sinai because of their sin. He was going to destroy them, until Moses prevailed upon God's compassion and forgiveness. But when he saw for himself that the Israelites were worshipping the calf and dancing gleefully around it, his anger burned and that temper took over. He threw the stone tablets from his hands and they broke. He burned the golden calf in the fire. The Israelites paid for their unfaithfulness, and once again Moses pleaded on their behalf.

He received the stone tablets a second time, but this time, when he descended from Mount Sinai, his face glowed from being in the presence of God and the people were frightened. Moses had to veil his face in order to avoid frightening his people. The timid shepherd who had quailed at the task set before him had become the man who stood in God's presence, who defended his people from God's just wrath and laid the foundation for a society that would be governed by laws and ruled by faith.

But the transformation was not complete. The Israelites, for their disobedience and refusal to believe that God's power could overcome earthly armies, had been condemned to wander for 40 years in the wilderness, until the generation that looked back to Egypt instead of forward to the future was deceased. A generation that owed fealty to God would enter the Promised Land. Moses' leadership encompassed a variety of roles as the Israelites made their way from slavery to freedom. But God had told Moses that he would not be the one to take the people to their new homeland. The prophet who taught his people to be a nation died on Mount Nebo, where legend says that his grave was dug by God. For the Jews, no other prophet compares to him.

The Israelites after Moses

Joshua became the leader of the Israelites after the death of Moses. He was a bold military leader and a confident believer in God, traits which the Israelites would need for the conquest of the Promised Land.

The conquest would involve bloodshed and miracles as the former slaves fought for their homeland. As soon as they crossed the River Jordan, they were headed for battle. They brought down the mighty city of Jericho with marching and trumpets, but the seven years of conquest would not always have miracles to count on. Without Moses to lead them, shield them, and intercede with God for them, the Israelites had to define who they were in a pagan land. The twelve tribes of Israel formed a union that owed its roots to the Patriarch Jacob, but in time, they would envy the other countries that had kings because their invisible God, no matter his might, was not enough. Their quest to keep up with the Joneses of the ancient world would ultimately lead to their downfall, despite the glorious reign of King David. It was at the time of their captivity during the Babylonian exile that their history was committed to writing. The Jews who returned from the exile rebuilt their temple and codified their beliefs. Moses was the foundation of those beliefs and for the Israelites, no other leader would match his achievements. Moses didn't just free the Israelites from Egyptian slavery; he gave them the law that would brand them as a people who knew God.

Why Moses Matters

Moses received the Ten Commandments from God; the first four commandments are based on religion; the fifth commandment concerns family responsibility; the sixth and eighth address the crimes of murder and theft; the seventh, ninth, and tenth focus on moral living: don't commit adultery, don't lie, and don't covet the belongings of others. It's a succinct body of law, but from it comes the foundation of our concept of justice and morality. The books of Deuteronomy and Leviticus provided more detailed laws for living as a people, but it's the Ten Commandments that altered history. They came down from Mount Sinai, they were held intact along with Christian precepts that would come much later. They traveled across oceans and seas, and took root in countries and continents far distant from the land of milk and honey where the Israelites would claim a home.

The legacy of Moses is lasting. For many, the Ten Commandments are the foundation of both personal and civil morality. Cases in the Supreme Court of the United States have cited the laws brought by Moses from God in legal proceedings. For American Founding Father John Adams, the Ten Commandments and the Sermon of the Mount, he said, "contained his religion."

U.S. President Harry Truman wrote in 1950 that the fundamental basis of the laws of the United States was the Ten Commandments that were given to Moses. "The fundamental basis of our Bill of Rights comes from the teachings we get from Exodus and St Matthew, from Isaiah and St. Paul."

The American Supreme Court pays tribute to Moses the Lawgiver. Above the back entrance where the Supreme Court meets, Moses is one of three figures in the frieze, taking his place in history for his bequest to humanity; he's holding blank tablets which bring to mind the Ten Commandments. Throughout the world, as laws are made and challenged, the contribution of Moses to the vitality of both legal courts and personal conscience remains a bulwark of jurisprudence.

Chapter Two: Alexander the Great

Who was Alexander?

Alexander, the Great never went to military school. But he had a pedigree that would be the envy of any West Point cadet, and a claim to fame that four-star generals would covet. This martial wunderkind was never defeated in battle. His native Macedon's boundaries were unable to contain him; Alexander conquered much of what was regarded as the known world at the time: Egypt, Mesopotamia, Anatolia, Syria, Phoenicia, Judea, and Gaza, reaching as far as India and covering 3000 miles of land. The only reason that his conquests ended at India was because his troops had had enough of wandering and battle, and they wanted to return home.

In the Beginning

Home was Macedon. His father Philip II was the king of Macedon; it was his principal wife, one of a handful of women also married to Philip, who gave birth to Alexander, on a memorable day when her husband had been victorious in battle. To make it a trifecta, Philip's horses had also been victorious, winning at the

Olympic Games. The queen decided that her son's birth, her husband's battle triumph, and Olympic laurels merited a personal response. So she gave herself a new name. Born Polyxena, the daughter of Neoptolemus, king of the Molossians, she had named herself Myrtale when she joined a cult, but Alexander's mother is most commonly known as Olympias, the name taken in honor of the king's victory at the Olympic Games of 356 BCE.

All of which sounds worthy of celebration, but the truth is that Alexander's royal parents were a tempestuous pair. Had they lived in modern times, their marriage would have made the front pages of the tabloids. In 337 BC, Philip took another wife, the niece of Attalus, a courtier of the king, and re-named her Eurydice. Their marriage was a political alliance, but there was passion between them. As it was, Philip's infidelities and Olympias' jealousy attracted sufficient notice to become notorious, creating reputations that have lasted for centuries. According to the 1st century biographer Plutarch, Olympias slept with snakes as a member of the cult of Dionysus.

Early Influences

Although Philip of Macedon had conquered the Greeks, he valued their training and intended his heir to benefit from Greek practices. Alexander was given rigorous physical training that emulated the demanding regimen of the warrior role models, the Spartans. As a royal prince, he was smart enough—the legendary philosopher Aristotle was his tutor from age 13 to 16 years and Aristotle's intellectual expectations were no less challenging than the physical ones the prince had undergone—and privileged enough to have chosen an easier life had he wanted to do so. But nobility in those ancient times did not necessarily promise a life of ease. In order to maintain what he was destined to inherit, he would need to defend it. The tempo of the times also meant that a leader had to expect that his lands would be coveted by others; a nation which had a powerful military man on the throne seemed more likely to thrive.

Philip was a warrior, and he would expect his son to follow his lead. But Alexander's gifts were not merely military. From an early age Alexander became the stuff of legend, some coming from a time when it was easy to believe that a youth so gifted was surely the offspring of the gods, perhaps even Zeus himself (a tale that might have flattered Olympias, but not necessarily Philip), and others from the boy's own remarkable exploits.

Nearly as famous as Alexander is his horse. The story says that one day, a trader brought a horse to court to sell, but the horse refused to accept a rider. No one could mount him. Recognizing such a beast as useless for his purposes, King Philip lost interest. But ten-year old Alexander proved himself to be an observant boy; he had noticed that the horse was frightened of its own shadow. Through careful training, gaining the horse's trust, and patience unusual in a child of that age, Alexander was able to mount and ride him. This stamina and insight would serve him well as the horse Bucephalus bore his master into battle in lands far from Macedon.

At 16, Alexander's education ended. Aristotle had taught him, as well as the youths who would become his generals, well. Alexander himself was a voracious reader, but the Greek philosopher also taught his students lessons which reflected the broad and expansive regard for knowledge which was characteristic of the Athenians: they learned philosophy and logic, science, ethics, art, and medicine. One hesitates to call Alexander a bookworm, but his parents were curious about his focus on learning rather than the wild oats that a typical young man would be sowing. When he was a youth, Philip and Olympias, concerned about the apparent absence of hormonal activity, arranged for a prostitute to entertain him, but Alexander did not succumb to her charms.

He was not ruled by amorous impulses. From the classroom, Alexander went to the battlefield, and when there was a revolt against the king, it was the king's son who put it down and named a city after himself, one of 70 that would bear his name. One of those cities would be Alexandria in Egypt, which would eventually be second in size only to Rome. Father and son went to war against their foes, defeating the Athenians and the Thebans and establishing an alliance with the intention of going to war against the mighty Persian Empire.

Father and son were brothers-in-arms, but as father and son, their relationship was often stormy. Alexander's position as heir depended upon his father's intention to keep him so, but also upon the absence of another claimant. Philip's marriage to a young woman of childbearing age brought those possibilities home when the bride's uncle, who also happened to be Philip's general, became drunk and, speaking unwisely, as wedding guests have done since time immemorial, voiced his hope that his niece would give birth to an heir. Not the kind of wedding toast that the current heir was likely to welcome. Alexander, along with his mother, Olympias, escaped from Macedon, but Alexander returned six months later when father and son had had time to calm down.

Alexander and Philip had more in common than kinship. They lived in a time when polygamy was accepted and bisexuality was a familiar tradition for young men. Alexander was deeply in love with the friend of his youth, Hephaestion, who had shared the classroom teaching under Aristotle's tutelage. Like Alexander, Hephaestion was a gifted soldier who rose through the ranks.

Alexander's Life Changes

Weddings and funerals brought out drama in the family, but weddings were not lucky for Philip. As father of the bride, he was assassinated at his daughter's wedding by one of his bodyguards, leaving his son Alexander the undisputed heir at age 20. There is some belief that Alexander's mother was aware of the plot against her husband and was not opposed to becoming the widow of King Philip and the mother of King Alexander.

Claiming the throne was one thing; keeping it was another. Alexander inherited an experienced and well trained fighting force and the young ruler had a naturally innovative sense of tactics in military matters. But his was young, and to enemies who were ready to pounce, Alexander was not seen as a viable threat. Consolidating a kingdom in the wake of a leader's death called for ruthlessness. First, Alexander had to clean house; that meant disposing of any potential rivals: family members, rival princes, and of course the rash general who had expressed his wish for a fertile marriage for the niece who had married Alexander's father.

That bloody duty accomplished, Alexander next turned his attentions to those conquered lands who thought that an untried youth would be easy to vanquish. The untried youth and his cavalry wasted no time in riding against the rebels. His shrewd strategy, remarkable in someone so young, brought the army to surrender. He defeated rebellious Thracians, Illyrians and Taulanti, then had to deal once again with Thebans and Athenians in revolt. Alexander had been injured during the siege of Pelium and the rumor of his death seemed credible enough, sufficiently credible to encourage Themes to revolt against their Macedonian overlords. Alexander had been relying on the presence of Macedonian troops to keep the Greeks in order, but he'd had to pull the troops when the Thracian and

Illrian revolts erupted. But Alexander's military acumen was already showing its prowess as he travelled 300 miles within two weeks, miraculously bringing his army undetected to the site of the battle under the very noses of his Greek enemies.

Wary of the Macedonian's skills, Athens and Sparta decided to play a waiting game. Thebes voted for war. Alexander was prepared to be lenient; if Thebes turned over the two men who had incited the revolt, no one would be hurt. Thebes issued a counter offer which was refused. This time, Alexander taught Thebes a lesson that was not lost on the rest of Greece; he burned the city to the ground. Those Thebans who weren't killed in battle were sold as slaves.

Alexander might have had an elite education, but when it came to warfare, he was no schoolboy. The Macedonian was intent on conquest. Next stop: Persia.

King Darius III of Persia was ready for the battle, with an army of perhaps as many as 200,000 soldiers to meet Alexander's 35,000 men (numbers are imprecise, but historians agree that Darius had a much larger force). With a tactical move that fooled the Persians into moving onto rocky terrain and away from the flat battlefield where they had the advantage, Alexander charged through the rear of the Persian army. Darius III was a craven king who did not fare well in martial exploits, and he fled from the battlefield. While it's true that the once-mighty empire was already showing signs of decay, Alexander's victories were no less significant. The conquest continued for several more years, but when Darius was killed in 330 BC, Alexander took his place as the Persian king. One more crown added to his collection.

There was, occasionally, time for less martial pursuits. As an adult, he eventually acquired a mistress named Campaspe, but a more lasting relationship was with a Persian noblewoman named Barsine, who bore him a child named Herakles in 327 BCE. Alexander's bisexuality did not diminish his reputation; Alexander believed in the bonds of marriage as a form of alliance. He ordered a mass wedding at Susa in 324 BCE, marrying the Persian King Darius III's daughter Statira and also Parysatis, the daughter of Artaxerxes III. His friend Hephaestion married Drypetis, the sister of the princess.

A man of Alexander's rank and stature was not confined by monogamy in either his male or female relationships. He entered a romance with a Persian eunuch named Bagoas after his conquest of the

Persians. There must have been affection between Alexander and Bagoas because when a Persian satrap derided Bagoas and refused to show him respect, Alexander had the satrap executed.

When Hephaestion died unexpectedly of typhus after the conquering of Asia, Alexander was devastated with grief. He ordered the death of Hephaestion's physician, spent a fortune on the funeral, and stretched his own body on the corpse for a day and night.

Alexander went on to conquer Egypt and Babylon. When his horse Bucephalus died in what today is Pakistan, Alexander named a city for him. Battle in India was to present a new threat in the form of war elephants. But once again, the Macedonians were triumphant. And weary.

The Macedonian military valued their leader. Alexander was not only skilled at warfare; he was a commander who bonded with his soldiers, knowing thousands of them by name. He shared the dangers of battle and the discomforts of the campaign. But while Alexander reveled in conquest, the Macedonians wanted more than endless battles and conquest; they wanted their home. They had followed him for 11 years, crossing 21,000 miles. India, hot and humid and very far from home, was ahead. At the Hyphasis River, the Macedonians told their ruler, their general, their companion, that they had had enough and would go no farther.

Alexander was not pleased with their mutiny, and sulked in his quarters like the mythological hero Achilles. But they would not change their minds. When he agreed to turn back, the army broke out in cheers and shouts of joy.

The man who conquered the known world would not live long to enjoy his efforts. In June 323 BCE, he attended a banquet and along with the other guests, took part in the bouts of drinking that followed. Feeling unwell, he went to bed, his condition worsening. Realizing that he was mortally ill, his soldiers wanted to see him for one last time. Although he didn't speak, he nonetheless acknowledged with a nod or a glance the soldiers of his army as they came to him. Ten days later, with a fever sapping his strength, Alexander died at the age of 33. Given the sanitary conditions of the times, historians deduce that the cause of death might have been typhoid fever or malaria. Of course, given the political climate of the era, it might also have been poison.

Alexander had spent his adult life in conquest, acquiring lands so that he could rule them and consolidate individual nations into one empire. But his death brought an end to the dreams of lasting empire. A king without an adult heir left a kingdom in jeopardy. Alexander was not a promiscuous man. His heart may have belonged to his longtime love, Hephaestion, but he had recognized his dynastic obligations. He had married three times.

His first official wife, Roxana, was the daughter of the Bactrian (Bactria was located in what is now Afghanistan) chief Oxyartes. Alexander had captured her during his Asian conquest, and married her in 327 BC. Her first pregnancy resulted in a stillborn son. Her living son, Alexander IV of Macedon, was born six months after Alexander's death. Alexander, the great warrior, had planned for conquest and empire, but he had made no contingency plans for an empire with an infant as the sole heir. Alexander did have a half-brother named Philip Arrhidaeus, but his sibling lacked the mental capacity to rule. Roxana, ambitious to secure her unborn child's position as heir, showed herself to be as ruthless and single-minded as her husband had been when she had her rival wives murdered. Statira, Alexander's second wife, and Hephaestion's widow Drypetis were put to death by

Roxana, who had their bodies thrown into a well that was filled up with dirt.

Her efforts were futile, as Alexander IV was murdered within a few years, and the empire divided up among Alexander the Great's generals. By 275 BCE, Alexander's empire had been severed into three kingdoms: Antigonid Macedon, Seleucid Asia, and Ptolemaic Egypt. Ptolemy, who had been one of Alexander's seven bodyguards, became the founder of Egypt's Ptolemaic dynasty. He realized early on that the vast empire Alexander left behind could not be maintained by a single leader. Egypt under the Ptolemaic kingdom was a centralized governing body ruled absolutely by its pharaohs. The city named for Alexander became one of the great cities of the ancient world, particularly known for its library, which housed 700,000 scrolls and the largest collection of books in that period of time, until a devastating fire destroyed the structure and its contents.

Macedon after Alexander

Alexander's incredible abilities made the Macedonian Empire the most powerful in the world, for a brief time at least. Alexander's embrace of Greek learning and customs became part of the country's identity, something that gained credence because of the renown of Aristotle, Alexander's tutor, whose teachings were carried on well after he was gone. However, Macedon without Alexander was prey to the military strife of the era. Macedon, Athens, and Sparta were in the throes of near struggles for supremacy; their weakness as a result meant that a united power would find them easy pickings. But as the Roman Empire gained power, Macedonian influence waned. In 146 BCE, the Romans conquered Greece. The Macedonians fought with the Romans and were defeated; the ruling dynasty was deposed and Macedon became a Roman province.

Why Alexander Matters

Ptolemy, one of the Macedonian generals, brought Alexander's body to Alexandria, where his tomb became a favorite destination for travelers of the ancient world, including Julius Caesar. The library at Alexandria was a great center of learning that celebrated the achievements of the Greeks and was a prized asset of the intellectual community until it was burned, centuries after Alexander's death.

Although the Greeks were conquered by the Macedonian father and son, Greek culture triumphed, and Alexander made no attempt to subdue it; he had a great regard for the sophisticated accomplishments of the Greeks. He brought his armies to the lands he conquered, but the spread of Greek culture would prove to be more enduring than his rule. Hellenistic ideals, philosophy, and learning, consolidated by the wandering conqueror, spread far across the subjugated lands. Western thought would be heavily influenced by the intellectual legacy of the Greeks.

With consolidation came expanded trade. No longer centered upon the eastern Mediterranean and Aegean Seas, new trade routes that followed Alexander's conquest incorporated Persia, India, and China. Trade between new partners of different ethnic heritages meant that ideas also followed the caravans. Greek thought spread rapidly and the Greek language became the tongue of the intellectuals. When the followers of a new religion based upon the teachings of Jesus Christ committed their works to writing, the New Testament of the Bible was written in Greek because it was the language known by the most people, far more than the relatively few who would have been fluent in Hebrew, the language of Christianity's spiritual forebears, the Jews.

Alexander and his armies carried the brain of Greek thought far beyond the borders of that influential island. As a result, the thousands of miles of land that he claimed would become a global community where trade and learning flourished, building a foundation for civilizations to come.

Chapter Three: Julius Caesar the Conqueror

Who was Julius Caesar?

Gaius Julius Caesar, unlike Alexander, was not born into the royal ruling family of his homeland. He couldn't have been; when he was born in 100 BCE, Rome was a republic, but it's through his drive, his military and political successes, his brilliance, and ultimately, his death that the Roman Empire was born. His parents were members of the aristocracy but the family was not wealthy or powerful. Rome had risen in influence thanks to its victory over mighty Carthage, but over the years, the aristocracy had earned the disdain of the peasant soldiers who made up the ranks of the army. Julius Caesar, unlike his more affluent peers, had a remarkable ability to take the public pulse, a talent that he might not have had if he'd been born into a more secure setting.

In the Beginning

Caesar's family claimed as an ancestor Aeneas, the famed prince of Troy and son of the goddess of love, Venus. Unfortunately, there was no legacy beyond divine antecedents for Caesar to inherit from this illustrious heritage. In fact, there was tremendous instability at the time of Caesar's youth and to be born into a family which, although noble, had no money or influence, was not the fast track to success. At the age of 16, his father died, leaving Caesar as the head of the family. The youth had a shrewd grasp of what it took to advance in society, even at his young age. In order to acquire rank and wealth, he married up, taking as his wife the daughter of Lucius Cornelius Cinna, a consul of the Republic. But when his father-in-law was killed after political setbacks and a mutiny by his troops, Caesar's political fortunes suffered as well. Nonetheless, he refused to divorce his wife.

Early Influences

Family could sometimes be a bloody business in those days; such was the case when Caesar was forced to flee upon being caught in a violent rivalry between his uncle and his uncle's enemies. It was time for a change of career, so Caesar entered the army. As the military assistant to a provincial governor, Caesar was sent to Cilicia. Legend says that in his next assignment, he was with the armies that put down the revolt led by the slave Spartacus. History would prove this to be a wise career choice, bringing prestige and fame to himself for his efforts.

When he left the army, he was still intent in improving himself and his prospects so he went to southern Italy to develop his skills in oratory. When he decided to leave for Rhodes, his ship was captured by pirates who held him hostage until a ransom was paid. During his time as a captive, Caesar's captors thought him a man of genial humor when he predicted that, upon his release, he'd have them all crucified. He was a man of his word; once released, he hunted them down and executed in the Roman fashion.

Caesar's career rebounded with another change in occupation: he turned to the law, prosecuting governors who were guilty of corruption and winning a reputation for his eloquence. Caesar's resume at this time showed a man who had a variety of talents that he employed whenever prospects looked dim in his current line of work. But when he was in Spain at the age of 30, he was said to have wept in front of a statue of Alexander the Great. By that age, the Macedonian had conquered most of the known world; Julius Caesar had a long way to go to match that achievement.

Because his father had often been away, it was Caesar's mother, Aurelia, who wielded the most influence on him, and when Caesar's wife Cornelia died in childbirth, Aurelia managed Caesar's households and took over the upbringing of his daughter, Julia. Aurelia Cotta's ancestry was more prestigious, with a family that could boast of some political influence.

Caesar's military career and political aspirations began to work in tandem; politics in republican Rome was not a game for innocents; when he campaigned to be a consul against two other candidates, bribery played a role. However, Caesar won. Now that he had power and influence, he formed an alliance known as the First Triumvirate with two powerful Romans, Crassus and Pompey. Immediately, Caesar made his move to gain allies among the people with a law that would redistribute public lands for the poor. A popular law, and one backed by Pompey's soldiers, was quite effective at winning support. Caesar's political career as a governor and his military career as a commanding officer successfully seesawed back and forth. Whether he was subduing aggressive tribes or conquering new territory, his reputation as a victorious military commanded was cast, and he added conquests in Britain and Gaul to his achievements.

Caesar's Life Changes
His former political allies, Pompey and Crassus, were

no longer part of the Triumvirate: Crassus was killed in battle, and Pompey had chosen an ally who opposed Caesar. The Roman Senate watched nervously and when Caesar returned to Rome, he feared he was going to be prosecuted. His bold decision to cross the Rubicon was more than a matter of geography; Caesar, knowing that he risked his life by doing so, crossed the river which served as a boundary of Italy, and brought civil war with him. With only one legion, Caesar defeated Pompey, who was later assassinated and beheaded, the head then presented to Caesar. It only took three months for Caesar to win control of the entire Italian peninsula.

Caesar's military acumen is undoubtedly one of his most famous attributes, but his relationship with the queen of Egypt occupied center stage, providing consuming interest today for audiences who may not be military enthusiasts but can't resist a scandalous love story. When Queen Cleopatra and her brother the pharaoh occupied opposite sides in a civil war, Caesar sided with the queen, defeated the pharaoh, and made Cleopatra the sole occupant of the Egyptian throne. Caesar's wife Calpurnia may not have been pleased at the very public relationship between her husband and the legendary Egyptian monarch, but there wasn't much that she could do about it. While Caesar's wife was expected to be above reproach, no such custom would inhibit her husband.

Cleopatra bore a son, named Caesarion, and when Cleopatra visited her celebrity lover, she stayed in his Roman villa. But Caesar was skilled at multitasking, so shifting from women to warfare was not a challenge. His military pursuits continued, this time to cement his authority against his rivals; he defeated Pompey's supporters and sons, and was appointed dictator for a ten-year term.

Rome was delighted to honor the conquering hero. For his part, Caesar had reform on his mind. He created a new constitution designed to fix some of the inherent weaknesses of the Republic, which had seen a devastating breakdown in the central government. In order to empower the government, he had to increase his own authority, which meant that other political offices saw their influence reduced. He celebrated his position in classic Roman style: the games for which Rome would become famous and then notorious, parades, gladiators, and mock battles.

Then it was time to get down to work. The census that he ordered meant that the grain dole was reduced. Families were rewarded for having babies, Caesar's method for increasing the population. He established term limits for governors. His debt-restructuring law eliminated approximately one quarter of all debts that were owed. He devised a plan to distribute land to thousands of veterans of his military campaigns. He created a police force, revised the tax system, rebuilt cities, and extended Latin rights throughout the Roman world. Mindful of his achievements, the Roman Senate gave the calendar a personal touch; the month of Quintilis was renamed July to honor Julius Caesar. He appointed new senators to fill the ranks of the reduced governing body, although its power was about to be diminished. He was given the power to veto the Senate. He began the process of transforming the empire into a cohesive unit, where Roman citizenship was a right given to both those who dwelled in Rome and those who were outside the city.

In 44 BCE, Caesar named himself dictator for life, which in effect gave him both executive and military rule, combining the dual roles for which Caesar had already proven his superiority.

But when the Senate honored him by issuing coins with his image, and a statue of him was placed next to royal statues, the supporters of the Roman Republic began to fear that Caesar's rise meant the Republic's downfall. Sixty members of the Senate who feared Caesar's power and imperial intentions determined that in order to save the Republic, Caesar had to be killed. They met in secret to devise a plan. Should he be thrown from a bridge during election time? Should the murder take place during a gladiator show? They decided that the most opportune site for the assassination would be in the Senate itself because the assassins could conceal their daggers in their togas, and there would only be senators in the chamber; no others were admitted.

According to accounts, Caesar's wife Calpurnia had had dreams warning her of danger to her husband and she begged him not to go to the Senate. Caesar himself had been feeling unwell and his doctors gave the same advice because he was suffering from the dizzy spells which frequently plagued him. But Brutus persuaded him to proceed to the Senate and not to allow the frivolous fears of doctors and his wife to dissuade him. A man of Caesar's renowned courage was unable to withstand this subtle argument, and he proceeded to the Senate.

Rumors were circulating of a plot against him; his right-hand man, Mark Antony, went to warn him, but was detained by the conspirators.

When Caesar arrived at the Senate on the Ides of March in 44 BCE, the senators rose when Caesar entered. The conspirators were at his side as he was approached by the brother of a man Caesar had exiled, who came near with a request. The assailants unsheathed their daggers and Caesar was stabbed multiple times by his assassins, each of whom wanted to strike a blow for what they perceived as freedom against tyranny; only the blow to the chest was fatal. Mortally wounded, Caesar fell, ironically falling to the floor at the foot of the statue of Pompey. The legend incorporated by Shakespeare that quotes Caesar saying, "You also?" to Brutus when he saw him among the assassins is probably a myth; the physician who attended him said that Caesar didn't speak while he was dying from his wounds.

The assassins expected the event to bring the city out in support; instead, the Romans hid inside their homes. Alarmed that the aristocrats had murdered Caesar, the ordinary people of Rome then turned their hero's funeral into an attack on the assassins. Civil war erupted and the Republic that that assassins thought they were safeguarding was destroyed.

Caesar's nephew and heir, Octavian, joined forces with Mark Antony and Lepidus, one of Caesar's commanders in the Second Triumvirate, which went the way of the first when Mark Antony and Cleopatra became allies and lovers who went to war against Octavian. This time, Cleopatra picked the wrong Roman. Military defeat at the Battle of Actium led to the suicide of the lovers. Antony and Cleopatra were immortalized in their deaths.

The Empire after Julius Caesar

The glory that was Rome overlooks an Empire that in the eyes of many sets the standard for imperial power and might, conquest and achievement, excess and vice. The men who ruled after Julius Caesar, some of whom were very capable leaders, some of whom have become bywords for, at best, incompetence and, at worst, depravity, knew the heights of power in their time. Roman military might was feared and respected for its discipline and where the army went, Roman order followed. True, dissent was not tolerated, but those were not tolerant times. The rise and fall of the Empire has been chronicled by the world's most eminent historians; its scandals are immortalized in television dramas. We know its playwrights, its architecture, and its historians. The Empire was brought down and other powers took its place, but the legend of the Roman Empire has never been surpassed.

Why Caesar Matters

Octavian took the name of Caesar Augustus and had his potential rival Caesarion, the son of Julius Caesar and Cleopatra, put to death. The Roman Empire was born and the heritage of Julius Caesar would resonate for centuries. A stable world made it possible for learning to flourish, and trade and exploration to advance. Caesar was not there for the most dazzling achievements of the empire, but without him, the glory that was Rome would not have blazed so brightly. Even when Rome fell, the legacy of its cohesion remained an example for Europe during the Dark Ages. Other empires fell into the dim past, forgotten by subsequent generations, but Rome and its leaders, their achievements and exploits, their boundaries and their legends, are remembered, as if the Romans defined what an empire was. If we only pay heed to the salacious events of some of the emperors which are gleefully recounted in cable television series and feature films, the achievements of an empire which spread its influence across three continents elude us. As it has for any entity which has the power to obtain whatever it wants, even if that power includes other people, imperial Romans did not practice an ascetic lifestyle. Caesar's machinations were the acts of a pragmatic, effective leader. But all his time was not spent wooing women, and the same is true for those who followed him in power.

The expanse of the Roman conquest meant that Latin spread as well, creating a linguistic legacy which endures to this day in the languages of Italian, Spanish, Portuguese, and Rumanian. The western alphabet owes its derivation to Roman letters as well. Julius Caesar was one man, and he was not an emperor, but his life set in effect the mechanism of imperial power which would dominate the map for centuries.

The legacy of the Caesars would resonate through history. The irony of the title is that the name Caesar is a nickname that probably meant "hairy." Gaius Julius Caesar would have been known as Gaius to his associates. Julius was his family name; the Julian family members were pedigreed members of the aristocracy. Since Gaius Julius was said to have a receding hairline, the hirsute adjective might have come from an ancestor who was blessed with hair. According to Suetonius the historian, Julius Caesar's baldness was a source of embarrassment for him and a source of amusement for his enemies who mocked him for his lack of locks.

But Gaius Julius had the last laugh as the name turned into a title; Gaius Octavius was renamed Gaius Julius Caesar Octavianus because he was Julius' adopted heir. Octavian emphasized the relationship by taking the title of Caesar; he in turn adopted his stepson, Tiberius, and renamed him Tiberius Julius Caesar. But by the time Claudius became emperor in 41 AC, Caesar was a title signifying the power and majesty of the ruler of Rome. The title would travel to other lands, including two that Rome did not conquer: when the Germans had a monarchy, the ruler was known as the Kaiser, derived from Caesar. Russia's ruler owed a linguistic debt to Julius Caesar. Rome never conquered the territory, but the czars of Russia controlled their country for hundreds of years until the fall of the Czar Nicholas II, the last of the Romanovs, who was assassinated in the early years of the 20th century.

But one of Julius Caesar's most famous achievement had nothing to do with the military or the Senate, or even his family, but does has something to do, even if peripherally, with his exotic Egyptian mistress. Just as the Republic had been in a state of chaos, the same was true of the calendar, which was based on the cycle of the moon. The Egyptian calendar followed the sun. Caesar adopted this calendar, known as the Julian calendar, which had 365.25 days in a year, with an extra day in February every four years. Empires fall, but time lasts forever.

Chapter Four: Jesus the Christ

Who was Jesus?

Jesus didn't have a seminary degree. For the first thirty years of his life, the family living came from carpentry, a trade taught to him by Joseph, his mother Mary's husband, in the town of Nazareth. So unimpressive was the little town that, when first learning of the new teacher who was attracting crowds of followers and seemed capable of doing amazing things, including miracles, one of the carpenter's future disciples said, "Can anything good come out of Nazareth?" But the man who died on Calvary's cross and left an empty tomb behind him brought truth to the prophecies that predicted the birth of a Messiah who would give rise to a new kingdom.

In the Beginning

By the time that Jesus was born, the Jews of the region had become accustomed to, although not fond of, the Romans who occupied their territory. Rome's advances across the map had seen the legions venture as far as North Africa, Asia Minor, what is today Turkey, and to Judea. King Herod was allowed to rule Judea in a semblance of independence, but the Romans were the ultimate authority. After Herod the Great's son

Archelaeus was removed as king by the Romans, his authority was given to the procurator or governor. That political role would have a dramatic effect on the final days of Jesus Christ; a man named Pontius Pilate was the procurator who would stand in judgment over the Galilean who was perceived as a threat to the stability of the region.

At the time of Jesus' birth, the region abounded with predictions of a Messiah who would rescue his people from their oppression and restore the land's lost glory. Herod the Great, learning from traveling wise men that a powerful king was to be born in his realm, certainly gave credence to the story. Herod was cunning, ruthless and paranoid. His response to this threat was to order the slaughter of all the male children under the age of two in order to get rid of the infant threat to his throne. But Mary's husband, Joseph, had been warned in a dream that the baby was in danger; the Book of Matthew says that the family went to Egypt. After Herod died, they went to live in Galilee, which, like the other regions where the Jews lived, was under the control of the Roman Empire.

The Jews detested the Romans who ruled over them. The Romans were pagan, for one thing. But that wasn't the only reason; when the Roman governor ordered a census, which was forbidden by the Jews—King David of old had been punished by God for initiating a census in his kingdom—a radical group known as the Zealots was born. The Zealots promoted armed revolt against the Roman Empire as part of their goal to attain self-rule and independence. When he began his ministry at the age of 30, Jesus would choose a disciple, Simon, who belonged to the Zealots.

Early Influences

Little is known of Jesus' early years, although there are stories from the Apocrypha which tell of his youth. The child born of prophecy and the Holy Spirit to a maiden named Mary, who was betrothed and then wed to a man named Joseph, came to adulthood in obscurity. If there was scandal attached to his birth because his mother was not yet married to Joseph, the accounts don't dwell on it although it would be surprising if the villagers did not.

Following the birth, Mary was required by Jewish tenets to go to the temple and present a ritualistic sacrifice which would remove the spiritual uncleanliness of childbirth. Anna and Simeon, two faithful Jews who were promised a sight of the Messiah before they died, were familiar with the historical accounts that a savior would arise from the house of David to rescue his people. They saw the family and the infant in the temple at Jerusalem soon after his birth. Anna was an aged prophetess of over 80 years who never left the temple. She thanked God for the baby, who she said would be the redemption of Jerusalem. Simeon foretold the blessings of the birth and predicts that through this baby would come salvation and revelation. Then Simeon gives the young mother a startling warning: Jesus would be opposed by many in Israel, and her soul would be pierced. From the time her motherhood began, Mary kept these words in her heart, and would see them come true when she saw her son die on the cross thirty-three years later.

These were dramatic events, but for the most part, the carpenter and his family lived their lives without attention. There was the episode when, at the age of 12, he and gone with his family to Jerusalem and, when he seemed to be missing, they finally found him at the temple. He seemed surprised by their concern, and said, "Didn't you know I'd be in my Father's house?" And then nothing.

Jesus' Life Changes
Jesus' mother is central to the story of his first miracle. Attending a wedding, Mary noticed that the family had

run out of wine. Jesus may have kept his identity and his destiny a secret from his neighbors, but Mary knew her son. She expected him to solve the problem. Jesus didn't intend to begin his ministry by rescuing a family from the ignominy of a failed wedding celebration, but his mother was practical. People who needed help needed someone to save them. And so it began, the ministry of Jesus of Nazareth, who turned water into wine at a wedding in Cana and later fed a multitude with five loaves of bread and two fish. He would go on to bring sight to the blind and restore working limbs to the lame. He would exorcise demons, halt hemorrhaging, and bring the dead to life. He saved a sinner from being stoned to death and praised the faith of a Roman centurion. He turned the world he lived in upside down, preaching of love and forgiveness. He called God "Abba" or Daddy, and would later infuriate the priests when he turned over the tables of the moneylenders because his Father's house was a den of thieves. He mystified people, and puzzled his own followers with his words and his predictions of death and resurrection.

He came from the line of David, the great Israelite king who had brought power and prestige to a people who were an afterthought among the mighty kings who shaped their destiny. They wanted another king, one who would throw off the hated subjugation of Roman rule, and oust the despised Herod family. They wanted a warrior and conquest and earthly power. That was not what the carpenter from Nazareth would bring.

The Galilean who chose fishermen, a tax collector and a political agitator to be his followers gave no indication that he intended to bring Jerusalem back to the glory days of David by wielding a sword. Quite the opposite. He was not afraid to tell people what they needed to hear, whether they wanted to hear it or not. He told the crowds who gathered to hear him preach that they should love their enemies, even the Romans. He told the local authorities that they were too tied to the letter of the law and too removed from its spirit. He told his disciples that if they wanted to do his will, they needed to become the servants of all. When the Judeans wanted to hear that they were God's favorite people, he told the story of someone, a hated Samaritan, who followed the word of God when a Levite and a Pharisee failed to do so.

Jesus' frequent contact with outcasts did not endear him to the religious authorities. Instead of rebuking sinners, he sat down at their tables in their homes and ate with them. He offered comfort and shared his teachings with the despised Samaritans, whose version of Judaism had been developed while the Jewish elite had been taken into exile in Babylon. There was considerable speculation and contempt for his treatment of women: in a time when females were personally insignificant and valued more as property than as individuals, Jesus included women in his ministry. And what a range of women! There were females of dubious reputation, including a woman of sinful repute who entered the home of a Pharisee where Jesus was a guest and anointed his feet with costly oils and then, using her hair, dried his feet. Instead of repudiating her, Jesus took the occasion to chide Simon, his host for having failed to offer the common gestures of hospitality. To Simon, Jesus was not a guest of significance. To the woman, Jesus was lord. Jesus used this episode to explain that great love inspired great forgiveness, no matter the number of sins. He told the woman that her sins were forgiven, but instead of rejoicing at this compassionate act, the guests were alarmed. Who did Jesus think he was to offer forgiveness to a woman whose offenses were repugnant to moral, upstanding members of society?

For three years, he taught and preached and healed out in the open, in full view of the religious authorities who feared his popularity and dreaded his power. He had followers in positions of power, but the momentum of his message was carried by the downtrodden and powerless, which were separated from God by the political and religious authorities who were an obstruction to God's comfort and healing.

There were even times in his ministry when he deliberately traveled with the idea of staying below the radar so that he would not be noticed. He often instructed the people he had healed to tell no one of the miracle he had caused. He knew that he was under surveillance by the powerful, who were waiting for proof of blasphemy so that they could bring charges against him. He knew that Herod Antipas, son of the tyrant who had murdered infants to safeguard his throne, was watching him; Herod had already executed John the Baptist for the prophet's bold words against the royal family. He knew that everything in Galilee was geared toward maintaining order so that Rome would not become alarmed. But Jesus was not afraid. He made friends of the Pharisees and adulteresses, he visited the homes of social outcasts, and he brought the promise of salvation to a population so accustomed to hopelessness that they hardly dared believe that change was possible.

But when Jesus upped his own game by raising a man from the dead, the religious authorities realized that here was danger that, as they saw it, threatened the safety of the Jews. Jesus had received word from good friends of his in Bethany, Mary and Martha, that their brother Lazarus was dying. Instead of hurrying immediately to heal the ailing man, Jesus lingered. When he finally arrived, it was too late. Lazarus had died, and his sister Martha did not mince words, laying the blame for her brother's demise upon Jesus. "Lord, if you had been here, my brother would not have died." When Mary met him, she levied the same accusation against him. Jesus could have prevented their brother from dying. They took him to the tomb where Lazarus had been placed. Their grief moved Jesus to weep. He ordered the mourners to remove the stone. Loudly, he called out for Lazarus to come out of the tomb. Emerging from the tomb was the dead man, now alive, still wearing the linen strips with which the dead were wrapped.

Word of this miracle, so much more powerful than any of the previous ones, soon made its way to the Pharisees. The matter was so monumental that the Sanhedrin called a meeting to decide what to do. If Jesus were allowed to continue his ministry, what would happen to them? If more people followed him, the Pharisees saw that their role in Jewish society would be threatened. The high priest Caiaphas made the final decision. It was better for one single man to die for the people, and for the good of the nation, than for many to die.

Jesus' fate was sealed. In the third and final year of his ministry, Jesus and his disciples entered Jerusalem, which Jesus had described as the city that murdered the prophets, to celebrate the Jewish Passover. If his fate had not already been determined, his actions at the temple would certainly have made him a target. Jesus went to the temple where the moneylenders exchanged currency so that pious and faithful Jews could offer sacrifices to atone for their sins. Jesus vented his outrage on the commerce which dominated the religious observations, overturning the tables as he charged them with turning the temple into a den of thieves.

But it was time for the Passover. His participation in this time-honored Jewish observance would be transformed into a sacred Christian ceremony, the Eucharist. Jesus broke bread and poured wine, enjoining the disciples to remember him when they ate the break and drank the wine. He washed their feet as a sign of servanthood, reminding them that God had called them to serve. But it was a tense meal; Jesus knew that his betrayer was among them. He told Judas

Iscariot, who had privately made arrangements to hand Jesus over to the religious authorities, to go and do what he had to do.

Judas led the priests and their entourage to the Garden of Gethsemane, where Jesus had spent an agonizing night in prayer, begging God to release him from the terms of engagement. Finally, Jesus surrendered to his fate saying, "Not my will, but Thine." Judas kissed Jesus to signal which of the gathering was the one they sought, and Jesus was taken to the high priest's house for interrogation. Following him from a distance was Peter the disciple, who feared for his life when he was recognized by the people outside the house. Peter denied that he knew Jesus, just as Jesus had predicted that he would do.

When Jesus was taken to Pilate, it seemed as if the story was over. Pilate found no fault in the man standing before him. When he learned that Jesus was a Jew, he sent him to Herod Antipas, but Herod sent him back. Trapped by the crowd now clamoring for a death sentence, and Jesus' silent refusal to mount a defense of his actions, Pilate ordered a basin of water to be brought. He washed his hands in the basin, symbolically absolving himself of the guilt in the sentence he was to render. Death by crucifixion on

Golgotha. Beaten and battered, Jesus hung on the cross for approximately six hours while the soldiers, waiting for death to come, gambled for his robe. When his body was taken from the cross, a follower, Joseph of Arimathea, had Jesus' body taken to a tomb that Joseph had intended for himself. No one had ever been placed in the tomb. The stone was rolled in place, and the story was over. But that was Friday.

When one of the followers of Jesus went to the tomb on Sunday, she didn't recognize the young man waiting there until he called her by name. He told her to tell his followers that he had risen, as he had promised, and that she had seen him and talked to him. The followers, hiding in fear that the murderous crowd would recognize them, were astounded and disbelieving at the story she told. Only when Jesus appeared to them did they understand what had happened. In the days after his resurrection, Jesus visited with his disciples, teaching them and eating with them as no ghost could have done, preparing them to carry on his work. When he left them, promising that the Holy Spirit would comfort them, all but one of them would be a martyr for the faith, preaching the gospel, baptizing believers, and building a new religion that faced persecution by Roman emperors and arrest by local authorities, all in the name of the Christ.

Christianity after Jesus

Jesus was the inspiration for the Christian faith, but he lived and died as a Jew. For decades after his death, the believers who followed a carpenter said to have risen from the dead were regarded as a sect belonging to Judaism. Jesus taught, preached, and healed in the land of his birth, but it would not be Jesus who would spread the gospel beyond the boundaries of Judea. The disciples he chose journeyed to other lands to share the teachings of Jesus, but it would be a man who never met Jesus who would be credited with making Christianity a religion that extended beyond Judaism. Paul, born Saul of Damascus, once a persecutor of Jews, would follow the scriptural instruction to go to the ends of the Earth and make disciples of all nations. Paul preached to the Gentiles, believing that they were worthy inheritors of the legacy of Jesus which had its roots in Judaism. He believed that Gentiles had something to contribute to the faith and they took to the new religion in droves. As their numbers grew and their practices began to differ from Jewish observances, the followers of Jesus Christ acquired a new identity and the name of Christian, as well as a reputation as troublemakers. To the Jewish authorities in Jerusalem, they were heretics who tainted the laws and practices that had been handed down from Moses. To the Roman authorities, these Christians defied the authority of Rome and denied the divinity of the emperor.

Why Jesus Matters

These Christians, as they came to be called, traveled from their homes to teach others about the carpenter from Nazareth. The world was eager to learn more. Converts were made wherever the disciples went. A new form of living was designed, one based on sharing rather than greed, and joy rather than selfishness. Persecution didn't diminish their numbers and even the violence of emperors like Nero and Diocletian failed to stop the growth of the new religion, which in the two thousand years since its beginning, now claims more than 2 billion followers, with new growth in Asia and Sub-Saharan Africa.

It was not a military conquest. But it was a conquest of souls.

Chapter Five: St. Paul the Evangelist

Who was St. Paul?

Saint Paul didn't have a television station that could reach multitudes with a Sunday morning broadcast. But his role in the growth of Christianity had an effect which supersedes the power of modern technology or televangelism. The man who would become a saint in the Christian church was born around 5 AD in the city of Tarsus, in Cilica, which is now Turkey. Tarsus was a seaport on the Mediterranean coast, so from his earliest days, he would have been familiar with the bustle of travelers and trade; this knowledge would come in handy for him later, for of all the disciples of Jesus, it would be Saul-known-as-Paul who would clock the most frequent traveler miles.

In the Beginning

The city of Tarsus was prosperous and well educated; the benefits of Greek knowledge which had come to the region in the wake of Alexander the Great had deep roots. Saul benefitted from the intellectual progress of his birthplace, but he also profited from something else; although he was a Jew, he was also a

Roman citizen. There would be times in Saul's future when the privilege of Roman citizenship would be an advantage, especially the right to a fair trial if arrested. Roman citizenship was greatly coveted in the Empire; to be born a citizen, as Paul was, was a singular achievement in a time when people paid a great deal of money for citizenship. Soldiers who served in the Roman legions for 25 years were eligible to become citizens if they were honorably discharged from service after that time.

Tarsus, which had first been conquered by Alexander the Great and later by Pompey, was designated a free city by Mark Antony because it had shown loyalty to him during the power struggles that erupted in Rome after the death of Julius Caesar. Its citizens were given citizenship because of the city's status; for Jews, this would have been particularly significant, since they could not otherwise have attained citizenship. Because Paul was a Roman citizen, he enjoyed the protection of the Empire; he could not be whipped by the authorities. He had the right to a trial before Caesar. Paul's Roman citizenship saved his life during his ministry, and forced the authorities to treat him with respect.

Early Influences

To grow up in Tarsus meant that Paul lived among a population that revered education. A philosopher from the city tutored Caesar Augustus when he was young, and served as his advisor when Augustus was the emperor. Paul grew up, received a sound education in the traditions of Judaism, studied under the Rabbi Gamaliel, and learned the trade of tent making. Birth and ancestry indicated that he would do nothing to venture outside the family expectations, but meeting those expectations would provide a life well lived.

Saul spoke fluent Greek, another advantage in the cosmopolitan world of his time. The man who would describe himself as the apostle to the Gentiles grew up as a faithful Jew, a member of the Pharisees, who strictly obeyed the laws of Moses. So from birth on, Saul was comfortable within the duality of the city in which he was born: the sophistication of a trade center where Greek philosophy and learning dominated, and the solid steeping in the faith of his ancestors.

Paul's Life Changes

However, his destiny was going to take him outside the familiar confines of his heritage. The evangelist to end all evangelists didn't start out as a believer in the controversial Galilean whose followers had aroused the wrath of Rome. Their adherence to a faith which failed to acknowledge the deity of the emperor provided bloody entertainment in the Colosseum, where citizens watched as Christians met their violent ends without recanting, bloodied but unbowed.

But life wasn't just dangerous for Christians in Rome. At this time, the Jewish authorities were dealing with what they regarded as a heretical sect that had followed the teachings of its leader Jesus, who had been executed by the Romans. There was plenty of danger right in Jerusalem, and Saul of Tarsus was one of the reasons why. Saul, who was proud of his Jewish heritage and his Roman citizenship, was zealous in his quest to bring followers of the blaspheming Jesus to justice. Christians feared him and those who hunted them down; they concealed their worship by using the symbol of the fish to indicate to others where followers could be found. These were perilous times for Christians when men like Saul of Tarsus were on the scent.

Damascus proved to be the undoing of Saul of Tarsus and the making of Saint Paul. As he traveled with his companions, a blinding light struck Saul and a voice that only he could hear demanded to know why Saul persecuted him. Saul, who persecuted Christians as a testimony of his fidelity to his Jewish faith, had no idea what the voice was asking, but as a sound Jewish scholar wise in the way of the holy books, he knew that his accuser was God.

Blinded and helpless, Saul was led into Damascus where he was tended to by a Christian named Ananias who must have been more than a little alarmed when he learned the identity of the man he had taken into his home, for Saul was well known to the Christian community. Saul had been present when the first Christian martyr, Stephen, was stoned to death for preaching that Jesus was the Jewish Messiah. But Ananias, whatever his doubts, did as he was ordained to do, and so the blinded persecutor was treated with compassion.

Saul recognized that, learned though he was, he still had much to learn. He was baptized, was renamed Paul and regained his sight. He went to Arabia for three years so that he could apply himself to his conversion to the religion that he had spent so much time and energy persecuting. His early preaching in Damascus and Jerusalem was not successful, as the Jewish persecution of the Christians was ongoing.

Throughout his ministry, Paul went on three

missionary journeys, traveling from Antioch to Syria, then westward through what is today Turkey and Greece, and then returning to Jerusalem where it all began. His training as tentmaker provided him work so that he could earn his living as he evangelized on behalf of Jesus Christ. It was when he traveled beyond the immediate boundaries where Christianity was a branch of Judaism that he found his calling. Paul's journeys to the lands where the gospels were unknown began to bear success. Paul was indefatigable in his zeal to preach the message that he had previously tried to stamp out, and as he preached and traveled, he wrote letters. Those letters to churches in Corinth, Philippi, Thessalonica, Galatia, Ephesus, Colossae, and to his fellow missionaries Timothy, Titus, and Philemon, make up thirteen of the books of the New Testament. But they're much more than just pages in a book. They provide the doctrinal background for the Christian tenets. The man who did not personally work with Jesus Christ, and who met him by way of a blinding lightning bolt, was the architect of the Christian faith.

Antioch, a thriving city which was home to a strong Jewish community, possibly as many as 40,000, was also cosmopolitan in its character. But as he preached the new faith to both Jews who were conversant in the doctrine in which Jesus had been raised, to non-Jews who had no background in either Judaism or Christianity, a source of friction emerged. Did Christians first need to become Jews? Circumcision was a time-honored tradition for Jewish males. There were certain foods which Jews were forbidden to eat. How could new converts to Christianity, which owed its foundation to Judaism, be accepted if they did not obey these teachings? For Paul, circumcision was no longer necessary to establish a covenant between God and his people, because Jesus had established a new covenant.

Peter, the disciple of Jesus described as the rock upon which the church would be built, had a dream. In this dream, he was told that nothing made by God could be considered unclean. The vision proved to the disciples that the teachings of Jesus could be embraced by gentile men and women. For Paul, this decision was his passport to preaching. Nothing stopped him, not pirates, storms, shipwrecks, or even arrests.

By this time, Christianity was identified as a religion separate from Judaism, and to be a Christian was to commit a crime. The new religion, which foretold of the coming of a new king and a new kingdom, was popular among the poor people of the city. Christians were not welcome in Rome, where imperial edict saw that them as troublemakers and treated them accordingly. But Paul knew that the path he had chosen was destined to collide with the worldly powers who regarded Christianity as a threat. He was summoned to trial in Rome. For two years he lived under house arrest, but that didn't stop him from expressing his beliefs. As his imprisonment continued, it was not safe to be seen in Paul's company or to visit him. A few of the faithful continued to maintain contact with him, including Luke, but although Paul felt the loss of company, his commitment to Christ was absolute. To die was to live in Christ. Paul was unafraid.

When the great fire spread through Rome in 64 AD, Emperor Nero blamed the Christians, and the persecution against them became even more virulent. The fire burned for a week and destroyed almost three-fourths of the city. Romans blamed Nero for the blaze, convinced that he had started it in order to clear land so that he could build his palace. It's little wonder that the Romans believed their emperor capable of arson on such a massive scale; in a time of imperial arrogance and cruelty, Nero is believed to have arranged the murder of his mother and his stepbrother. While some of the accusations may be based on rumor, it's true that Nero punished Christians for the fire by ordering them to be burned and crucified.

Sometime around the mid-60s AD, the Emperor Nero ordered Paul's death. Because he was a Roman citizen, Paul was not crucified. Instead he was beheaded. It's believed that Peter was also killed during this time; tradition says that Peter chose to be crucified not upright, as Jesus had been, but facing down, because he did not deserve the honor of dying as Jesus had died. For believers, death was not something to be dreaded. For Paul, it was time for him to be with Jesus, as he was eager to be.

Christianity after Paul

Christianity had the advantage of rising in a time when Roman order made travel and the spread of ideas more accessible. Just as the Roman legions marched from the empire's capital to the far reaches of the Mediterranean, Christianity made its way to converts far from Jerusalem. But the hostile atmosphere that martyred the original disciples and brought Paul to death did not ease when Nero died. There were years of brutal persecutions ahead. But Paul's determination to bring the Gentiles into the fold of faith proved to be the religion's rescue. Christians would eventually know the safety of the government, with protection coming from none other than a Roman emperor named Constantine.

Why Paul Matters

Thirteen of the twenty-seven books of the New Testament are authored by Paul, and he plays a dominant role in another book, The Acts of the Apostles, which tells the story of the birth of the Christian church. Paul's writings created the foundation for Christian theology. His transformation from a persecutor of the sect into the energetic and indomitable architect of its growth into a major religion made him the right candidate to address the nonbelievers and Gentiles. Paul's educational background provided the means for him to interpret the stories and teachings of Jesus into theology that made sense of the life, death, and resurrection of an itinerant Galilean preacher. His familiarity with the Greek language and thought made him capable of translating the teachings and writings into what was the universal language of the era. His reference to Jesus as "the Christ" is the Greek translation of the Hebrew word for "Messiah" and it delivers the message of Jesus to a broader audience that would have had minimal familiarity with Jewish tradition.

Although centuries have passed since Paul's death, the effects of his life can still be witnessed. The Christian faith grew and thrived in places that owe their numbers to the fact that the man from Tarsus accepted the call to be the apostle to the Gentiles. Had evangelism remained in Jerusalem, or only been extended to followers of Judaism, the sect would never have become a global faith practiced by people of all ethnic origins.

Chapter Six: Constantine the Great

Who was Constantine?

The Emperor Constantine, also known as Constantine the Great, didn't give any early signals that he would be one of those men so revered that he would end up with an adjective following his name. But during his life and long rule, his military successes and his administrative skills created stability in the Roman Empire. His decision to convert to the Christian religion that previous emperors had persecuted was a dramatic one, lodging the faith in the centers of power and promoting its growth and development.

In the Beginning

When Flavius Valerius Constantius was born in 272 AD to an officer in the Roman army and a woman named Helena who may have been a concubine, not a wife, the Roman Empire had changed from what it was under Caesar Augustus. Helena was of low birth, some accounts claiming that she was possibly a stable maid, but a union with her was not a way to marry up. There are legends that claim that she came of royal British stock and that she was the daughter of the British King

Coel. What is certain is that Constantine's mother was a remarkable woman whose role in the development of Christianity is significant; she was named a saint in the Orthodox, Roman Catholic, and Anglican Churches.

But in the perilous political atmosphere of Rome at this time, she was merely a woman of no great importance. It was believed that the real work of the world was done by men; women sat on the sidelines. Yet one wonders how much of Helena's beliefs influenced her son; the evidence seems to bear out the belief that she did much more than watch life pass by. She was no spectator.

Before young Constantine was much older, circumstances would change even more. The empire was ruled by co-emperors, with Diocletian reigning in the East and Maximian in the West. The split was not a hostile one; although each emperor had his own court, military and administrative centers, there were no restrictions on their movements. When his father Constantius was made a deputy emperor under Maximian, later marrying the emperor's stepdaughter, he left Helena. After the divorce, or separation from Constantius, she and her son Constantine, with whom she had a close bond, were sent to Diocletian's court.

Early Influences

Constantine's early life was lived in the midst of domestic conflict, political turmoil, and religious violence. During this time, persecution of Christians by Diocletian was particularly ruthless, nearly three centuries after the religion had been born. What was known as the Great Persecution lasted from 303-311, as Christians once again were served up as entertainment for bloodthirsty crowds. Christian property was destroyed, and their holy writings burned. Constantine's mother was a Christian, although there's no record of when she converted, or whether the state persecutions placed her in any danger. Whether she covertly practiced her faith or had not yet chosen it, her imprint would leave its mark on her son's nature.

Constantine's Life Changes

The complicated politics of the empire directly affected Constantine. Co-emperors Diocletian and Maximian abdicated in 305, but when Constantine's father did not succeed to the imperial throne, he summoned his son to be at his side as he went to war. When Constantius was killed, the army declared Constantine as emperor. Constantine had the will and the skill to make that declaration a reality.

Military skill undoubtedly played a part in his battles, but for Constantine, his victory at the decisive Battle of the Milvian Bridge was a crucial turning point in the lives of Christians. Before the battle, Constantine had a dream. He was to paint the Christian symbol, the Chi Rho, on his soldiers' shields. Another story says that Constantine saw the symbol appear in the sky along with the words, "In this sign, conquer."

In 313 AD, a year after his victory at Milvian Bridge, Constantine met with the co-emperor Licinius to develop a policy regarding religion in an empire that was home to many varying beliefs. Licinius was a pagan, but Constantine by this time was already showing signs of support for Christianity, although no one knows for sure whether his beliefs were deeply rooted.

Although there had been a gradual movement toward tolerance of the Christians, the emperor in the East, Maximinus Daia, had resumed the persecutions and Christians continued to be imprisoned because they were seen as disloyal and offensive to the Roman gods. The Edict of Milan, the work of Constantine and Licinius, which ceased persecution of Christians, and returned the property that they had lost during times of persecution, promoted religious tolerance, not only of Christianity but of all religions. Christianity did not become the official religion of the empire until much later, but religious tolerance was a dramatic change from state-sponsored persecution. Constantine wanted to be on good terms with any divinity that could have an effect on his battles, so he was intent on not offending any of them. However, he felt that Christianity, with its positive emphasis on morality and simple living, could serve as a unifying force that would stabilize the empire.

The empire was in need of stabilizing; it had been embroiled in civil war for 20 years. The architects of the Edict of Milan remained political rivals and in 324 AD, Constantine defeated Licinius. Constantine's sister, the wife of Licinius, pleaded with her brother to spare her husband's life. And Constantine commuted execution to imprisonment, but when he learned that Licinius was conspiring to return to power, he and his son were executed, along with the Emperor Martianus. Victorious, Constantine reunited the divided Roman Empire into one

Upon becoming emperor, Constantine summoned his mother to his court. Helena was already a member of the Christian sect, so some of her son's willingness to adopt the new religion may have come from her influence. Helena lived to be 80 and among her achievements were her Christian faith and her pilgrimage to the Holy Land. After Constantine appointed her as Augusta Imperatrix, he provided her with funds to find religious relics. Religious relics are difficult to authenticate, but Helena researched her findings, listened to the stories of the people whose families had lived in the area for generations, and possibly, returned with items which actually came from the life of Jesus. She ordered the building of the Church of the Nativity and the Church on the Mount of Olives, where Jesus was born and the site of his ascension. When she found a temple on the site of what was purported to be Jesus' tomb, she ordered it torn down.

Military leaders from pagan times have long credited their victories to divine intervention, so this reaction by Constantine would not of itself have been remarkable had he not carried through with his conversion. He donated land for the building of a cathedral and began to pass laws that provided Christian clergy with legal privileges. Crucifixion was replaced by hanging as punishment. Sunday became an official day of rest; this was when Christians began to celebrate the Sabbath on a different day instead of sharing the Jewish Sabbath. Gladiator games were no longer allowed. Prisoners had to be allowed to spend some time outside in daylight and were no longer solely relegated to total darkness.

Under Constantine, one of the roles of the emperor was to define heresy and orthodoxy. This role would expand as the Empire weakened and fell as a political power, but later saw Rome turn into the ruling center of Christianity. In 325 he opened the Council of Nicaea to settle issues of heresy which threatened the young church in a very different way from what persecution had done. At issue was the nature of God. Debating the matter were bishops, many of whom had survived persecution under Emperor Diocletian and had faced death rather than surrender their beliefs.

It was at this council that the Trinity was codified, and God the Father, God the Son, and God the Holy Spirit established as Christian doctrine. Constantine recognized that these unresolved issues were a threat to the stability of the empire, and the maturing of the church directly affected the citizens who were now ruled by a Christian. Was Jesus more human, more divine? Was he God's equal? The priest Arius believed that Jesus was created; others said that Jesus was and always had been eternal. Arguing against Arianism was Athanasius, the Bishop of Alexandria, from Egypt. In response, the bishops at the council wrote the Nicene Creed, which states that Jesus is fully divine. The issue was not resolved by this first meeting of the Council, but the Nicene Creed remains, along with the Apostles' Cred, one of the core affirmations of faith in Christianity. It was at this Council that Sunday was designated as the official day of Christian worship, although some Christian groups had already changed the day of the Sabbath from Saturday to Sunday.

When Constantine went to Rome in 326 to celebrate the 20th anniversary of his accession to the imperial throne, he offended the Romans by his refusal to participate in a pagan ceremony, which would argue for the sincerity of his dedication to the Christian faith. But it's important to remember that, although a ruler might adopt religious tenets and endorse a particular faith, he may not always find it expedient to completely live out the beliefs that he professes. And an emperor's life was constantly engulfed in plots, machinations, political backstabbing and ambition on the part of rivals. Even a ruler's domestic life was not without discord.

This was lived out in the emperor's own life when Constantine had the deputy emperor executed. The deputy emperor, Crispus, was Constantine's son by his first wife. Crispus had been reared to rule; like his father, he was a skilled military leader who apparently showed much promise as a future emperor. His education came from a learned scholar named Lactantius, who was a Christian. He and his half-brother, Constantine II, were given the title of Caesar. Crispus was given an army and a staff and assigned to administer Britain, Gaul, and Spain. He performed his duties well and showed himself as the inheritor of his father's military acumen when he defeated the Franks and the Alamanni in 320 AD. His naval victory in the Second Licinian War contributed to his father's triumph. But all those achievements seemed to pale in comparison to the charges, still unknown, which were made against Crispus; in 326 AD, Constantine's decree was carried out and Crispus was executed. Constantine and his heirs kept their secrets, and history is not sure what happened in the family that led to the execution of Crispus.

It's said that Constantine's mother, Helena, was the one who told her son that he had erred in executing his eldest son, and that in truth, Constantine's wife Fausta was the culprit. Fausta was the daughter of the Eastern Emperor Maximian; she had been given to Constantine in marriage in 307 AD. Fausta had formerly been held in high regard by Constantine, perhaps in part because, when her father Maximian was involved in a plot to assassinate Constantine, Fausta revealed the plot to her husband, saving his life. In 324 AD, she was given the title of Augusta as proof of the trust that Constantine had in her. By giving birth to three sons, she solidified Constantine's continued claim to the throne.

But Fausta's sons by Constantine would rule only if his eldest son, Crispus, was not the heir. There is speculation that she was intensely jealous of her stepson, but also that she was committing adultery with the young man. Another story holds that she accused her stepson of rape. Other accounts say that she had made the claim that her stepson had forced a girl to become his concubine against her will, an act which would offend the Christian emperor.

The reason for the executions may not be confirmed, but stories agree that Fausta met her death, either by suffocation or scalding in an overheated bath, by order of the emperor. Later, regretting what he had done to his son, he erected a golden statue of Crispus. Constantine had his wife written out of the official history, and although the sons she bore to Constantine eventually rose to the throne, their father's edict was never revoked.

Constantine's domestic changes were followed by geographic ones. The city of Rome was too far in distance from the armies and the frontiers. In 330 AD, Constantine established a new capital, turning the village of Byzantium into Constantinople, symbolizing the break from the Empire's pagan past and transformation into a spiritual center. In his new capital, which was easier to defend, he could enjoy the wealth of the region. Constantine forbade the celebration of any pagan ceremonies in his new capital. The earliest extant Christian Bibles were delivered to the Church of Constantinople. For 1,000 years, Constantine's city would stand as the capital of what remained of the Roman Empire.

In 337, when Constantine realized that death was near, he wanted to be baptized in the Jordan River, because that was where Jesus had been baptized. But he was too ill, and instead was baptized on his deathbed. Legend claims that the reason he had held off from baptism for so long after his conversion was to allow himself the freedom to continue sinning, since the belief at the time held that sins committed after baptism would prevent him from going to heaven. He died wearing not the royal purple, but his white baptismal robe. May 21, the day he died, is celebrated as a major feast day in the Orthodox Church.

The Empire after Constantine

Constantine's decision to center his empire in the East proved to be a wise one. The Western Empire was not what it was in its heyday. In 476, Rome fell. It would revive as the center for the Christian faith, where the pope held vast power over the faithful of Europe. In many ways, the pope was just as imperial as his royal predecessors, dictating to kings, summoning soldiers to war, dictating peace terms and authorizing marriages. Continuing as a secular entity, the Eastern Empire where Constantine established his center of power survived long afterward, well into the Middle Ages.

Why Constantine Matters

Constantine died a Christian, but old habits are not easy to leave behind, even as death is imminent. The Roman Senate elevated him to the status of deity, as had been the custom for the previous pagan emperors. But history remembers him as the emperor who chose to be a Christian. Because the religion was elevated to imperial status, Christianity benefitted greatly. The religion had the backing of a powerful emperor, and the administrative support of a solidly structured organization. The Nicene Creed was an early effort to define theological issues that threatened the wellbeing of the church, and the Edict of Milan promoted religious tolerance in a time when tolerance of any sort was rare. But Constantine's contributions as emperor didn't merely stabilize Rome through his religious beliefs. Had he remained a pagan, his military achievements alone would have made him a memorable ruler. The solidus, the coin that he introduced, was a currency standard for 1,000 years. He was an emperor made to last, and his administrative, financial, and military reforms strengthened the empire.

Chapter Seven: Muhammad the Prophet

Who was Muhammad?

The man who brought Islam to the world did not expect to be known by 99 names, but today he is revered by Muslims as the Prophet Muhammad. Pagan Arabia was transformed into the center of the religion of Islam; after Muhammad's death, Islam would travel to Asia, Africa, and parts of Europe. The Prophet was himself a modest man who did not claim his achievements for himself, but as the workings of Allah.

In the Beginning

This descendent of Ishmael, the son of Abraham by Sarah's maid Hagar, was born in 570 AD in Mecca, a member of an influential and prestigious tribe. Within six years, his mother Amina, and father Abdullah, and his foster mother would be dead, leaving him in the care of his grandfather and uncle, Abu Talib, a camel herder with some social standing, who raised him. Very little is known about his early life. The Quran is a holy book and not a biography of the Prophet, so missing details about his years before his revelation from the Angel Gabriel will not be found. In some ways, it's as if his life before he became the Prophet sent by Allah was not of significance; after Islam, however, the world would never be the same.

Early Influences

Deprived of his parents at such a young age, Muhammad was dependent upon Allah, a state which Islamic scholars believe was the beginning of his future role as the messenger of Allah. Islamic scholars have compared the trials of Muhammad's early life to those of the Jewish prophet Moses.

The Arabian Peninsula was a barren land, isolated from the intellectual ideas which spread from the West. Its isolation protected it from armies of conquest as well; the population owed its loyalty to the respective tribes in the region. At this time, Arabia was characterized by pagan religions, with idol worship a common practice. Historical records provide few details of this time, but Christians and Jews in the area believed in one God, so there was acknowledge of monotheism which Muhammad would reinforce when he became the Prophet of Islam.

When he was around the age of 12, he traveled with his uncle to Syria, where he learned about the prosperous trading that was thriving in the Middle

East. The trade routes were well established and profitable; later, they would prove to be useful for the spread of Islam, as traders and believers brought their faith with them as they journeyed. But the founding of Islam was still some years away and Muhammad was still a boy. Nonetheless, a Christian monk named Bahira prophesied that the boy would be a prophet.

His experience as a camel driver led to a career managing merchant caravans. Middle Eastern caravans were part of the prosperous spice trade, as Europeans learned that pepper, cinnamon, nutmeg, and ginger could flavor food and were also regarded as medicinal. For Muhammad, travel along the trade routes introduced him to people of all nations and religious beliefs. Muhammad was in a unique situation for the times, because his boss was a woman of means. She was a wealthy widow who might have heard that Muhammad was known as al-Ameen, meaning honest, reliable, and trustworthy. Although she was fifteen years older than he, the couple married when Muhammad was 25. The proposal came from Khadija, and was delivered to the young man via a relative. Together, they had six children; the four daughters survived, but the two sons died at very young ages. Managing her trading business meant that Muhammad frequently traveled, and as he journeyed to other areas, his experience and knowledge broadened. The business was a profitable one, and the marriage was a happy one, so happy that, although there were no laws against polygamy, Khadija was his only wife until she died at the age of 64.

When Muhammad was 35, a dispute broke out in Mecca. The town leaders were in disagreement over which clan should have the honor of setting a sacred stone on a building known as the Kaabah, a cube-shaped building which would come to be regarded as the house of Allah. Finally, unable to solve their quarrel, the leaders decreed that the next man who walked through the gate would make the decision. Muhammad was that man; he spread a mantle on the ground and placed the stone in the center. He had the leaders each lift a corner until the mantle rose to the height he needed. Muhammad then put the stone in place.

Muhammad's Life Changes
Muhammad was clearly destined for greatness, but greatness can be disconcerting. Khadija must have been a remarkably intuitive woman, for when Muhammad was 40, he returned home after a day spent in contemplation in a cave on the outskirts of Mecca to tell her that he had been visited by an angel.

She believed him and took him to her cousin, a Christian who was knowledgeable in holy writings. When Waraqah ibn Nawfal heard Muhammad's account of what had happened, he confirmed that his experience matched scriptural accounts of prophethood. Khadija's cousin also warned him that prophets were often unwelcome in their communities, and predicted that his own people would cast him away.

Muhammad explained how he had been visited by the angel Gabriel, who instructed him with a single word: Proclaim. The angel told Muhammad to read, but Muhammad was illiterate. That did not dissuade the angel. Like many holy men, Muhammad was reluctant and only gave in when the angel relentlessly continued to issue his command. It was from the Angel Gabriel that Muhammad received the first verses of the Quran. His mission was to bring a halt to the idolatry which characterized Arab society at that time in Mecca.

After repeated visits from Gabriel, Muhammad realized that he had been designated to be a prophet. Like Moses, Muhammad was reluctant to accept the calling. But his resistance was not strong enough to withstand the insistence of the angel Gabriel. His mission was to direct the sinners of his country to worship Allah and turn away from their sinful ways and their multiple gods. The Quran does emphasize Mohammed's moral character as a human being; no divinity is ascribed to the Prophet, but he is set apart as a model for other Muslims to follow.

At the end of three years of prophecy, he had gained 40 followers. In the fourth year, Allah ordered him to extend his proclamation to the public, and to stress the oneness of Allah, justice, and the last judgment. During his years of proselytizing, followers of this new faith were subjected to prosecution and violence and even imprisonment. One of the tribes, the Quraysh, proposed a form of worship which was not permitted by the Quran.

But news of his ministry had spread to the city of Yathrib, 280 miles north of Mecca, where feuds were a constant source of instability. They had planned to restore peace by nominating a leader to take charge, but some people found the prospect of a leader like Muhammad to be promising. A delegation from the city asked him to come there to lead them. If they did so, the delegates vowed that they would give their worship to Allah alone and obey Muhammad. It was an incredible offer, fraught with opportunity, but also peril, because Mecca was by no means willing to let him go.

A search party left Mecca to find him, but Muhammad, along with his friend Abu Bakr, was able to make his escape in 622. This is the beginning of the Muslim calendar, and the escape is commemorated as the Hegira. Yathrib received a new name, Medina, becoming the first Islamic state. There had been fighting between the pagans and the followers of Judaism for over a century.

Muhammad's new home suited him. He was able to bring together the city's tribes, which included followers of Judaism, into a cohesive unit which was able to function despite their differences of origin. Tribal in-fighting had contributed to the violence which dominated Medina. Muhammad's Constitution of Medina or the Medina Charter brought the Muslim and Jews together in an alliance which outlined the rights of the communities in the city. The role of the charter was to create what was designed to be a collective Islamic state, comprised of multiple religions, in Medina. Eight groups who practiced Judaism were included in this charter of remarkable tolerance. Muhammad was designated as the mediator among the nine tribes and held the ultimate vote when a situation called for a declaration of war. Establishing religious tolerance was central to the purpose of the charter. The representatives of all the groups, both

Muslim and otherwise, were included when decisions were to be made.

The charter has a significance which expands its role in bringing religious tolerance to disparate groups. Muhammad affirmed the bonds of faith above the traditionally powerful ties of kinships.

Key components of the charter included the following precepts:
- The security of God was the same for all groups
- Non-Muslims had the same political and religious rights as Muslims
- Non-Muslims would equally share in the defense of the state and the cost of defending it
- Non-Muslims were not required to participate in religious wars in which Muslims engaged

After the departure of the Muslims from Mecca, the Quraysh leaders subjected remaining new Muslim converts to persecution. Their caravans incited the neighboring tribes against the Muslims. Although the Quran held that war was wrong, it was permissible for those who had been wronged to fight to defend themselves. Muhammad proved his diplomatic skills by negotiating treaties with the tribes to protect Medina from attack, persuading the Quraysh trade caravans to compromise, and helping Muslims in Mecca to evacuate.

But his success in Medina stirred up problems with Mecca and conflict ensued. Muhammad's emphasis on social and economic justice and the need to share one's belongings with the less fortunate threatened Mecca's business ventures. The Meccan army was much larger, but the Medina forces prevailed in their first battle in 624. In 628, Muhammad called upon the leaders of other lands, asking them to join the Muslims in worship of Allah; his invitation was accepted by the rulers of Byzantium, Persia, Ethiopia, Egypt, Syria, and Bahrain.

There were other battles between the two cities; Muhammad was wounded in one of them, but in 630, Muhammad's army defeated Mecca and witnessed the conversion of the Meccan population to Islam. Muhammad destroyed the city's pagan idols, but did not retaliate against the Meccans who had opposed him. Instead, he offered amnesty to anyone who had transgressed against Islam or done an offense to him. The Meccans expected violent retaliation against them for their years of persecution against Muslims, but Muhammad explained that he would treat them as the Prophet Joseph had treated his brothers, returning kindness and love for their ill treatment of him.

He continued his work as a spiritual leader, while also serving Medina by initiating social and religious reforms. Muhammad and family members lived simply without ostentation. He would spend from one-third to two-thirds of each night in prayer and meditation. Following the death of Khadijah in 620, Muhammad added more wives and concubines to his household. His wives were called "Mothers of the Believers" who were devout followers of Islam. Two of his wives were prisoners of war; marriage to Muhammad gave them protection and stability.

Islam after Muhammad

Muhammad died two years after the battle of Mecca. After Muhammad's death following a long illness, the question of who should succeed him arose. One group felt that the successor should be chosen by the Muslims. Another group thought that Muhammad's son-in-law, Ali, who had married Muhammad's daughter Fatimah, should take the leadership position. The Shia wanted Ali to fill Muhammad's position so that the leadership could remain within the Prophet's family. The Sunnis wanted the leader who was deemed most suitable by the community to become Muhammad's replacement. When the Sunni faction won, they chose a successor who became the first caliph. Ali was eventually named the fourth caliph, but violence bloodied the movement; two of the earlier caliphs were murdered and in 661, after becoming caliph, Ali was killed in the fighting. Ali's son, Hussein, continued the war as leader of the Shiites. He met the caliph's army in battle and was killed, along with 72 members of his family and his companions. The two groups have never resolved their religious differences and continue to oppose one another.

Why Muhammad Matters

The faith Muhammad had founded was thriving and within two years after his death, all of the Arabian Peninsula was Muslim. He received the Quran, the holy book of Islam, over a period of 23 years, as the messages from Allah were revealed to him. For the world's two billion Muslims, the Quran is a book of holy revelation which guides them in their faith practices. Known as the Five Pillars of Islam, faith, prayer, charitable giving, fasting, and the pilgrimage to Mecca are at the core of the Islamic beliefs governing the lives of the faithful.

Islam spread by military expeditions to Egypt and North Africa, but also through trade. The caliphs who led the faith after his death were successful in spreading the teachings of the Quran, and within a century, Islam had stretched to the Atlantic and the borders of China. Under the influence of the caliphs, schools were established which taught the Arabic language. The caliphs also began to build mosques, creating structures which would endure for centuries.

In time, the faith would spread far beyond its homeland, to bring comfort to believers all over the world. But the followers of Islam and the followers of Christianity clashed in Spain, France; they fought over the Holy Land, and for centuries the believers described, along with Jews, as the People of the Book, displayed hostility toward each other. The irony is that the religions which preached peace and love adopted weapons of war as they fought the battle of their gods.

Chapter Eight: Napoleon the Emperor

Who Was Napoleon?

The Emperor Napoleon Bonaparte didn't have a drop of royal blood in his veins. The French over whom he ruled may not have minded; he brought to an end the bloody carnage of the French Revolution and put civil order in its place. If the royal French dynasty which met its demise at the blade of the guillotine was replaced by a Corsican soldier who came from a large and opportunistic family, all of whom would profit from Napoleon's rise, at least he brought the French more land and glory.

In the Beginning

But the man whose name became synonymous with an empire was actually born of Italian ancestry, in 1769. His name was Napoleone di Buonaparte, but with an eye to the future, he renamed himself Napoleon Bonaparte to have a more French-sounding name, since Corsica, his homeland, was under French rule. Actually, France had acquired the island from Genoa, an Italian city-state, in 1768, the year before Napoleon was born. Nonetheless, his spoken French always bore a noticeable Corsican accent, and his French spelling was imperfect. His family heritage was actually of the aristocracy, if not exalted. Carlo and Letizia had a large family, with five sons and three daughters who survived birth, and his uncle was a cardinal.

The France of Napoleon's youth posed a sharp contrast between rich and poor. Wealth and power were clustered in the hands of very few, while the majority of the French lived in poverty. Employment options were limited, and for people who lived in the cities, merely feeding their families drained their few resources. France itself was hostile to them: the water was dirty, the air was unclean, and disease spread quickly and fatally in crowded urban areas. But the desperate circumstances of the poor in France were a matter of either disregard or ignorance for the wealthy. Marie Antoinette probably did not respond, "Let them eat cake" upon learning that the peasants lacked bread, but the famous quote illustrates the disconnect between the rich and poor. Disregard for the plight of the peasants had been a habit for so long that it seemed ingrained in the 18th century version of lifestyles of the rich and famous. But the time was coming when desperate times would lead to desperate means, and France would explode in civil war. And when that happened, Napoleon Bonaparte would be poised to step in and bring order to the chaos.

Early Influences

Napoleon received his education at a military academy, where he was enrolled at the age of 10. He excelled in his studies, showing a natural ability that led to his transfer to the Royal Military Academy in Paris. He graduated at the age of 15, having finished a three-year course of study in a single year. He served in an artillery regiment for several years until the outbreak of the French Revolution in 1789. Within three years, the revolutionaries had declared France a republic and overthrown the monarchy. Napoleon supported the revolution and also supported Corsican nationalism. He took leave—two years of it—as the fighting in Corsica raged among the supporters of the Revolution, the monarchy, and Corsican nationalists. He rose to the rank of captain in 1792. While back home in Corsica, he made connections with a political group that supported democratic rights and had a disagreement with the Corsican governor. In 1793, he and his family moved to France, where, a month later, he earned the support of the brother of Maximillian Robespierre, one of the founders of the Revolution. The civil chaos of the French Revolution provided the ideal setting for a man of skill and ambition who had managed to rise through the ranks in the military. His plan for the capture of the city of Toulon earned him a promotion to the rank of brigadier general when he was 24 years old.

Politics is always unpredictable, no more so than when a civil war is raging. The master of the Revolution, Robespierre himself, fell from power in 1794, leaving Napoleon without an influential protector. For a short time, Napoleon was placed under house arrest. But Napoleon was a survivor, and he was asked to devise a military strategy to attack Italy as part of France's war with Austria. When an assignment to the Army of the West threatened to demote him from his rank as artillery general, he claimed that health issues would not permit him to accept.

But all was not spit-and-polish military tactics during this time of upheaval. When Napoleon was transferred to the Bureau of Topography of the Committee of Public Safety, he found time to write a novel about a soldier, probably based upon his romance with his fiancée Desiree Clary, whose sister had married his brother Joseph. Napoleon the romance writer is not one of the attributes for which he is typically acclaimed, but he was a man of versatile talents.

Napoleon's career prospects at this time looked bleak. His ploy to avoid serving in the Army of the West led to his removal from the list of active service generals. But Napoleon had the ability to bring victory to his side. He was given a command position to defend Paris against a royalist rebellion in 1795. Obeying Napoleon's command, one of his officers fired the cannons, killing 1400 of the royalists. Napoleon was promoted to the rank of major general, given command of the Army of Italy, and then he married Josephine de Beauharnais, a sophisticated widow six years his senior.

The six years' difference in age may not have been significant, but Josephine was much more experienced than her young husband, and was not inclined pay heed to the commandment against committing adultery. Napoleon's passion for his wife was recorded in his letters, which reveal how much he missed her, how much he treasured her letters, and how very much he wished that she would join him. Napoleon's jealousy would ease in time, while Josephine's conduct would turn more circumspect, but the presence of other lovers had altered their relationship.

But while he was a soldier, he was with his army. His soldiers defeated a larger Austrian army in 1796; the following year, the defeated Austrians signed the

Treaty of Campo Formio which left the French with more territory gained from their victory.

When the subject of invading England was proposed by the Directory, which was the group of five that had been in charge of the French government since 1795, Napoleon didn't want to test the French Navy against the powerful British Navy. He decided to invade Egypt instead, to employ a subtler attack against the British by threatening their trade routes with India. He was able to conquer the Egyptian Mamluks in 1798 at the Battle of the Pyramids, and to bring legal reforms to the nation, as well as introduce Western culture. Early the next year, however, his invasion against Syria, which was ruled by the Ottoman Empire, failed. But when it was apparent that he would not be able to weaken the British trade routes, he returned to France, where the scene was ripe for a man of action.

Josephine had been busy laying the groundwork for his return. As a hostess, she invited influential people to their home so that she could lobby for the role her husband could play in a new France. But the troubles between the two led to estrangement. And then reconciliation. When he returned to their home, the couple exchanged accusations and tears, ultimately leading to reunion. Bu the emotional balance had changed; Josephine became the faithful wife, but for Napoleon, the rules were different. Before too long, he would no longer be discreet.

Napoleon's Life Changes

Nor was he inclined to be cautious. He took part in a coup d'état that overthrew the Directory, which was replaced with a three-member Consulate. Napoleon was made first consul, setting the stage for his political rise. His victory over the Austrians in 1800, driving them out of Italy, boosted his image and his power. In 1802, the French and British signed a peace treaty. The treaty would only last a year, but it was apparent that the Corsican general was not a foe to be taken lightly by the other European powers.

Military endeavors took up much of his time, but so did stabilizing the government which had been undermined during the years of revolutionary rule. He was able to institute banking and educational reforms and also to improve relations with the Pope; relations had suffered due to the revolutionary government's abandonment of religion. Interestingly, Napoleon himself, although a Catholic, was broadminded in religious matters. His time in Egypt had introduced him to Islam, and Napoleon memorized parts of the Quran as part of his admiration for the Prophet Muhammad.

He became first consul for life in 1802.

However, when it was time for a coronation, Napoleon followed tradition. Napoleon I was crowned Emperor of France in 1804 at Notre Dame Cathedral.

An emperor needs an heir, and Josephine had not provided one. He had his marriage to her annulled, and went royal-wife shopping, deciding on Marie Louise, who was the daughter of the Austrian emperor. A year later, Napoleon II was born. The old revolutionary ideals of life without aristocracy were gone as Napoleon created a new aristocracy. It was lucrative to be a friend of the Emperor Napoleon, even more advantageous to be a relative, and as he conquered countries, more thrones were occupied by Bonapartes: Louis became the king of Holland; Jerome of Westphalia, Joseph of Naples and then Spain.

Napoleon's ambitions for conquest had the European powers worried, but the warfare that threatened Europe was a boon for the young country across the Atlantic Ocean. In order to raise funds to pay for his wars, Napoleon sold France's Louisiana Territory to the United States for $15 million. The bargain meant that the United States paid approximately three cents per acre for the vast expanse of territory that almost doubled the size of the country.

In 1805, Napoleon was the victor at the Battle of Austerlitz, defeating the Austrian and Russian armies. His victory brought an end to the Holy Roman Empire. But in that same year, his navy was defeated at Trafalgar by the British. But he was the dominant military master of Europe, defeating the Russians in 1807 and the Austrians in 1809. He continued to wage economic war against the British by blockading European ports against British trade. His victories extended French domination over what is today Holland and Belgium, along with significant amounts of Italy, Germany, and Croatia. Switzerland and Poland were under his rule, as was Spain and some German states. He had defeated Austria, Prussia and Russia.

As famous as Napoleon is for his victories, it's his defeat by the Russian winter that also remains in the minds of historians. France had defeated the Russians in war, but Czar Alexander I, who had refused Napoleon's offer of one of the Bonaparte sisters in marriage, was displaying signs of resistance. The Russians imposed a hefty tax on French lace and other luxury exports. Alexander was concerned that by creating the Duchy of Warsaw, which was carved out of Prussian territory, the Poles would become hostile and fall under the influence of nationalist rebellion. His Grande Armee, the largest European armed force that had been brought together up to that date with at least 450,000 soldiers and possibly 650,000 was not defeated in battle.

Napoleon invaded Russia in the summer of 1812, but within six months, freezing temperatures, lack of sufficient food, diseases such as typhus and dysentery, and Russian attacks nearly destroyed his forces. The Russians, with only 200,000 soldiers, retreated whenever the French moved to attack, luring the army ever deeper into the country as the months moved forward. To keep the French from living off the land, the peasants burned their own crops. Without the ability to replenish his supplies, Napoleon had no choice but to retreat, losing almost half a million soldiers to death and capture in the Russian campaign.

The Russians and French did meet in combat at the Battle of Borodino; casualties were enormous and the Russians withdrew, leaving Moscow undefended. When the French entered the city on September 14, it was in flames. The Muscovites had fled, leaving only their liquor behind. The French took advantage of the alcohol and ransacked the city. But when Alexander I failed to approach Napoleon with an offer of peace,

Napoleon, his army now numbering only 100,000 troops, pulled out of Moscow.

The retreat was humiliating and disastrous. The troops were attacked constantly on the flanks and rear guard, there was little food to plunger, and a frigid winter set in earlier than usual. There were stories of soldiers heaping corpses in the windows to shield the living from the sub-zero temperatures and snow. Thousands of wounded French soldiers were left behind. When Napoleon heard rumors that there had been an attempted overthrow of his government in Paris, he left the command of the army under Joachim Murat and returned home.

The brilliant general who seemed immune to defeat was proven to be human after all, and Europe's leaders took note. His enemies—the Spanish, Portuguese, British, Austrians, Prussians, Russians, and Swedes— found that it was prudent to join forces against him. Once again, Napoleon raised an army but the losses in Russia had left his military force without much experience. He was defeated in 1813 at the Battle of Leipzig. By March of 1814, Paris had fallen. Napoleon was exiled to the island of Elba off the Italian coast. His mother and sister Pauline joined him and his mistress visited, bringing their illegitimate son with her. For news about his son and heir, however, he was obliged to write to his wife, Marie Louise; she did not join him in exile.

He ruled over a shrunken kingdom of 12,000 inhabitants, and did actually apply his administrative abilities to improving the conditions on the island for its residents by building hospitals and seeking ways to making potable water more available. He continued to receive letters from all over the world; he read international newspapers and kept abreast of events in the world. The newspapers revealed that, following his exile, a pro-Bonapartist movement had sprung up in France. But the leader who had conquered Europe was not likely to be content with an insignificant island kingdom for long. Although he was under the watch of Austrian and French guards, he found a way to escape from Elba and make his way to Paris in 1815. The crowds in France cheered for his return. King Louis XVIII fled to Belgium. The French police who were sent to arrest him instead supported his cause. Napoleon moved back into the Tuileries Palace and turned his attention to governing, promising to develop more reforms to bring democracy to the French. The aristocrats were dubious about his return; they were less than enthusiastic at the prospect of more reforms and his promise—or threat, in their eyes—to establish a constitutional government.

The European powers who had exiled him were stunned by his escape. Once again, the military conqueror was at war. But his initial success was short-lived, and he was decisively defeated at Waterloo in 1815. This time, he was exiled to a bleak, barren, island located in the southern Atlantic Ocean. His home had not furniture, shutters, or curtains on the windows. The single room would serve as his bedroom, dining room, study, and sitting room; when it was time to clean the residence, Napoleon had to go outside. From the splendor of his palatial living he was now reduced to bread and wine which were much reduced in quality. According to a member of his entourage that accompanied him to St. Helena, even the water, coffee, butter and oil were unfit for use.

Six years later, Napoleon died. He wanted to be buried in France, but it wasn't until 1840 that his remains were brought to Paris, where he was interred along with other military heroes.

Because samples of his hair contained high levels of arsenic, some people were convinced that he had been poisoned. But an autopsy determined that he died of stomach cancer. The presence of arsenic was apparently not uncommon in those times, and there was some evidence that his sister Pauline had also succumbed to cancer.

France after Napoleon

Weary of war, and determined to avoid domination by another military conqueror in the future, the Quadruple Alliance, which consisted of Great Britain, Austria, Russia and Prussia, sought a return to the way things were before, when there was a balance of power among the nations, or at least the nations who were the chief players in European politics. In order to restore order, the Bourbons were returned to power in France. France was required to return to its 1792 borders, to pay 700 million francs, and support an army of occupation of five years. This clemency toward France was inspired less by an attitude of forgiveness than by the conviction that the ideals of the French Revolution which had led to upheaval and bloodshed had included egalitarian philosophies would thrive if France were punished for Napoleon's acts. But the restoration, and the return to power of the Catholic Church, could not undo all the changes wrought by the French Revolution and Napoleon. Social advances had been made, and the Bourbons ruled as a constitutional monarchy. By supporting the restored monarchy and King Louis XVIII on the French throne, Europe's powerbrokers intended to nurture peace on the continent. By agreeing to meet together out of common interest, this "Concert of Europe" helped discourage international conflict during the 19th century. The 20th century, of course, would tell a very different tale.

Why Napoleon Matters

While Napoleon's military campaigns continued to be studied in military schools all over the world, his civil achievements have had a more lasting effect. Under his rule, divorce was legalized, religious tolerance was established, and feudalism abolished. The Napoleonic Code is more than a reference by Stanley Kowalski in the play *A Streetcar Named Desire*. Established in 1804, it endorsed freedom of religion and determined that government employment should be given to the most qualified and not to those whose relatives were the most influential.

Napoleon's work in reforming France's legal system was not an easy task. Frances's laws consisted of local customs and special charters granted by the monarchs. When the French Revolution did away with the remaining remnants of feudalism, the way was cleared to establish a modern civil code. Laws were clearly written. They were applicable only if they had been officially published, abolishing the practice of secret laws, or laws that applied to events taking place before the law was established. Blasphemy, heresy, sacrilege, and witchcraft were decriminalized in the new penal code.

An emperor without a blue-blooded pedigree, a military genius who was inspired by conquest, and an able administrator who wiped up the blood from the French Revolution and dusted the cobwebs off the outdated French government apparatus, Napoleon was a symbol of the changes that were brewing in the world.

Chapter Nine: Gandhi the Mahatma

Who was Gandhi?

Mohandas K. Gandhi was born in India in 1869, the son of an Indian political official and his fourth wife. He would become famous for the simplicity of his life, his steadfast beliefs in peace and nonviolence, his commitment to tolerance, and his dedication to the country of India, for whose independence he endured arrests, imprisonment, and beatings. His practices would influence leaders in generations to follow, teaching leaders that patience and the practice of civil disobedience could be more effective than guns in achieving political goals.

Early Influences

At the time of Gandhi's birth, the British had held influence in India since 1599 when the British East Indies Company established a profitable trading business. As the centuries passed, the business enterprise become more political until eventually the British were in control of India. In 1857, just 12 years before Gandhi's birth, the Great India Mutiny erupted;

the British quelled the revolt but it was an indication that the Indians were weary of their status as subordinates in their own country. The independence movement was not predominant, but the Indian National Congress, formed in 1885 when Gandhi was a teenager, would begin to seek more rights for Indians and eventually independence.

Gandhi's home was in Porbander, in a coastal area where he lived not only among the Hindus, but also Muslims. His father, Karamchand Gandhi, welcomed Muslims as guests in his home, demonstrating to his son that tolerance toward others was part of one's moral duty. Putlibai Gandhi was a woman whose life was based upon her religious beliefs and service. Practicing the faiths of Hinduism and Jainism, Gandhi grew up believing in nonviolence, fasting, tolerance of others, a simple lifestyle, and vegetarianism.

Piety was stressed in the household, but not education. Gandhi went to school, but he was a mediocre student. Gandhi was married at the age of 13 to a 14-year old girl named Kasturbai Kapadia, but she was called Kasturba. Gandhi recalled his wedding day as an occasion to dress in new clothes and eat sweets. Marriage at such a young age eventually would eventually cause Gandhi to realize that child marriage was a hardship for women, although the tradition for the young bride was for her to spend more time at her parents' home and not with her husband. Their first child was born in 1885 but died within a few days. Gandhi felt that the death of their child was his punishment for leaving his father's death bed so that he and his wife could have sexual intercourse. Gandhi later explained his sense of guilt. "I felt deeply ashamed and miserable. I ran to my father's room. I saw that if animal passion had not blinded me, he would have died in my arms." The couple would eventually have four sons.

Gandhi was not a success as a student, but he decided that he wanted to be a barrister, which meant that he would need to go to England. He had to promise his mother that he would abstain from drinking wine and eating meat, as well as becoming intimate with other women. Maintaining a vegetarian lifestyle in England in the 19th century was a challenge, but he found a vegetarian restaurant, and became a member of the London Vegetarian Society. His conviction against eating meat would become one of the building blocks of his activist lifestyle, and he was transformed from a backward and shy young man into someone willing to speak out on behalf of what he believed.

He returned to India, where his career in law was not successful, so when he was hired by a Muslim firm and offered a position in South Africa, it was a good opportunity for him to develop his professional skills. It's ironic that the man who would confront and best the mighty British Empire was actually too timid to be an effective lawyer in a courtroom. What Gandhi and the world didn't know then was that it wasn't his legal talents that would make his mark in the world.

Gandhi's Life Changes

But nonetheless, his introduction to discrimination began immediately. When railroad officials on the train told him to transfer to third class, Gandhi, who had first-class tickets, refused to move and he was forced to leave the train. He discovered that this was not uncommon, and then he had to decide whether to return to India or stay in South Africa and fight. For two decades, Gandhi worked as an advocate for Indian rights, becoming a prominent leader in South Africa's Indian community.

The issue for Gandhi was to decide how to fight the discrimination that he realized was rampant. Under his leadership, the Indian Congress began its opposition to segregation. He opted for the concept of satyagraha, which means truth and firmness, in order to combat the treatment faced by Indians. Also known as passive resistance or civil disobedience, his campaign would require tremendous fortitude. His commitment to religious tolerance was strengthened by his conviction that Indians needed to support one another regardless of what religious faith they practiced.

His revolution was not an intellectual protest. Gandhi numbered laborers, miners, and agricultural workers in his ranks. When he led a march of over 2,000 people into the Transvaal to protest a tax levied by the British against people of Indian heritage, he was arrested and sentenced to nine months in prison. By 1913, many of the Indians in the community had been jailed, beaten, and shot. Gandhi's wife, Kasturba, was part of the movement and was sentenced to three months of hard labor for her role. But finally, the South African government made some concessions, including the abolition of a poll tax which Indians had been obligated to pay. His fame spread across the international stage

As Gandhi's political consciousness grew, his spirituality became more pronounced. His mother had been much given to prayer and fasting, and her example was followed by her son, who eventually became known as Mahatma or "the great-souled one" for his commitment to a life dedicated to service. In his 30s, he embraced poverty and celibacy as a way of life, going so far as to encourage his fellow Indians to avoid marriage, but if that was impossible, to abstain from sexual relations as husband and wife. His support of chastity was not without controversy as, later in his life, he encouraged young women to sleep and bathe with him while naked, but with no sexual interaction. Gandhi wrote that his wife agreed to this decision to be married and celibate; the leader's wife did not personally refer to their celibate marriage.

1914, the same year that World War I would break out in Europe, Gandhi returned to India. But thanks to his advocacy of Indian rights in South Africa, his eyes were opened to the discrimination that native Indians suffered in their own country. He began to notice that the treatment of Indians under British rule was not always fair to the people of his country. But when he announced a protest against a law which allowed the British to imprison anyone suspected of terrorism, the day turned violent; 400 were killed and 1300 were wounded. The violence made Gandhi's thoughts turn toward Indian independence.

By 1920, he was committed to Indian independence from Great Britain. His leadership in the Indian

National Congress spurred the movement toward independence. Again, his plan of action focused on nonviolence and civil disobedience. But in order for a country to be independent, the nation needed to develop its own resources. India's fate had been tied to Great Britain for centuries, and those bonds would not be easy to break. Validated by the Indian National Congress, the independence movement led to boycotts of British manufacturing. He encouraged Indians to develop their own products for use and export, including homespun cloth.

The British charged him with sedition and sentenced him to two years in prison but he was released two years after he began serving his sentence because he needed surgery for appendicitis.

Gandhi would not condone violence, and when the independence movement used violence, he called an end to the resistance.

However, he returned to political activism with renewed vigor in 1930 with a campaign against the salt tax which the British government, with its monopoly on salt, imposed upon Indians. The British forbade Indians from collecting salt; instead, they had to buy British salt, which included a large tax. He began his campaign just months after the Indian National Congress declared independence. He traveled 24 days on his march to produce salt without payment of the tax, attracting a growing number of Indians as he progressed along the March to the Sea. Defying the British order, the Indian protesters boiled salt water to make salt instead of buying it from the British. The movement was a magnet for Indians who began to embrace the idea of independence. Gandhi was arrested, but his wife Kasturba continued on the march; she too was arrested.

But the arrests didn't stop the movement. The Congress Party staged a satyagrapha at the Dharasana Salt Works, which continued for nearly a year. Even when they were physically attacked, clubbed, and beaten, they did not resist or strike back. When the British finally gave way on some points, although not all, Gandhi called off the protests. The British were forced to allow Gandhi to take part in a conference to discuss the future of India. Gandhi recognized what had happened; speaking to a crowd, he held a handful of salt and told his audience that, with that salt, he was shaking the foundations of the British Empire.

Unfortunately, the British were unwilling to accede to the Indian demand for independence. Indians who were Sikhs and Muslims did not have faith that Gandhi was able to fairly represent the needs of nonHindus.

Gandhi began to notice discrimination not only on the part of the British but within India itself. He went on a series of hunger strikes because of the way the Hindu untouchables, the poorest of the poor, were treated, forcing the Hindu community to bring about some reforms. The Indian Muslims, a minority in the Hindu country, felt that their voice was not being heard. Gandhi himself was tolerant of all faiths, convinced that every religion deserved to be equally represented. He explained that when he was young, he had tried to combine the diverse religious teachings of the Hindu *Gita*, Edwin Arnold's acclaimed account of Buddhism in *The Light of Asia*, and the Christian Sermon on the Mount.

Intending to focus on the plight of the Indian poor, Gandhi resigned from the Congress Party but when World War II broke out, Indian independence was once again an issue of pressing concern. Prime Minister Winston Churchill wanted Indian support, but to Gandhi, it was wrong of Great Britain to expect Indian assistance when the British kept Indians in a state of subjugation in their own country. Gandhi opposed Nazism; he offered cooperation with the British in exchange for their withdrawal from Indian. India was a vital ally during the war, strategically due to its proximity to the South-East Asian theatre of the fighting, but also in manpower. But the "Quit India" campaign that demanded that the British leave ended up with the leaders of the Congress Party imprisoned in 1942. While he was in detention, his wife joined him, and died in 1944. Gandhi was released a year earlier due to his health.

When the war ended, India had emerged as a nation whose political and economic resources had to be reckoned with. The Congress Party, the Muslim League, and Great Britain began the negotiations for independence. India was split into two segments, with the nation of Pakistan formed for the Muslims. India was independent, but not on its own terms. Partition was controversial, and rioting broke out as 10 million people migrated to the new nation. Gandhi spoke out to protect the Muslims who had elected to remain in India in support of Muslims and Hindus living in peace, Gandhi went on a hunger strike.

Gandhi lived his life according to a policy of tolerance to all, but not everyone in his country approved of his tolerance toward others. He was on his way to a prayer meeting on January 30, 1948, when he was assassinated by a Hindu fanatic who was enraged by Gandhi's tolerance of Muslims. One million people made up the funeral procession as his body was carried through the streets of Delhi.

India after Gandhi

India under the British Raj was not a paradise. Independence brought the nation the right to govern itself, but the deep-rooted religious divisions between Hindu and Muslim led to the partition of India and Pakistan. The separation was violent and the split uprooted many. India was challenged to fortify the ideals of the revered Mahatma while sustaining a path of political progress. The country's first Prime Minister, Jawaharlal Nehru, did not have the iconic status of Gandhi, but he was committed to protecting the rights of the weak, supporting the rights of women, and easing the plight of the untouchable caste. Demonstrating the strides that India made in its advancement, Nehru's daughter, Indira Gandhi (no relation to the famed leader), would eventually become prime minister at a time when countries with a longer history of democracy did not grant females equality in the political sphere.

Why Gandhi Matters

Gandhi is known as the Father of Indian Independence,

a title he richly deserved. India today, with its population of one billion people, is the world's largest democracy, a nation that has found a way to combine economic vigor with democratic principles. But Gandhi's influence extended beyond the borders of India. Martin Luther King, Jr, the American civil rights leader, became aware of Gandhi's commitment to nonviolent protest while he was a seminary student. Almost a century later, a South African man who had once employed violent means to fight against the policy of apartheid decided to adopt nonviolence. He was held under house arrest for 27 years, but ultimately, Nelson Mandela and his peaceful noncooperation ended apartheid in the country where Gandhi had achieved his political baptism.

THE END

**** PREVIEW OTHER BOOKS BY THIS AUTHOR****

[Excerpt from the first 3 Chapters – for complete book, please purchase on Amazon.com]

"BUDDHISM FOR BEGINNERS" by Dominique Atkinson

Chapter 1: Introduction

Buddhism is considered one of the first organized religions arising in the 4th and 5th centuries. With a following of approximately 300 million people around the world, Buddhism was founded approximately 2,500 years ago by Siddhartha Gotama, known more commonly as Buddha. Though it is generally considered to be a religion, Buddhism is more accurately a way of life, leading its followers to be moral, mindful and full of wisdom and understanding. In doing this, followers of Buddhism aspire to attain enlightenment and live a truly fulfilled life.

Buddhists are constantly surrounded by statues of Buddha. These images are used to remind all followers of the level of peace and happiness that they can achieve through enlightenment. Though followers may appear to worship these idols, what they do is actually pay their respects to a man who become more than just a man; someone who they believe is the true key to their enlightenment.

Although many viewing Buddhism from the outside believe he was God, returned to Earth, this is not the case. He never claimed to be God and instead believed himself to be merely a man who was capable of achieving enlightenment. He was determined to help anyone and everyone (no matter what their background or demographics) achieve enlightenment.

One of the best things about this philosophy or lifestyle is that it is tolerant of all others. Under Buddhism other religions and belief systems are not only tolerated, but accepted and believed in. It actually believes in the teaching of all religions and does not seek to convert those who are presently following other religions. Instead, it only seeks to explain Buddhism to those who are interested in learning it, leaving all others to their own devices, beliefs and religions.

These beliefs definitely make Buddhism very different from most other religions which have spent time, energy and even money in converting others to their beliefs and ideals. There have never been wars or battles fought in the name of Buddhism because acceptance, tolerance and love are taught so strongly as basic tenants of the religion.

Chapter 2: The History of Buddhism

Buddha was born in Nepal in the 6th century B.C. Siddhartha was born to a tribal king. His mother passed away only shortly after his birth. He was shut away in a beautiful palace with only servants to keep him company. Though he was married at the age of 16, he continued to live in seclusion for 13 more years.

The myth is that when he was finally allowed to leave the palace in a chariot, he was amazed and surprised to see so many examples of humanity that had before been kept from him. The first thing he came across was a very old man, to which his chariot driver explained that everyone grew old. Upon another trip outside he came across a diseased man, to which his driver explained, people would grow ill throughout life. A subsequent visit introduced him to a decaying corpse, introducing the understanding that people would someday die. Finally, he was introduced to an ascetic, someone who had given up all worldly things and, simultaneously, fear of death.

He was 29 by this time and decided that he would become an ascetic as well. Leaving behind his beautiful palace and his family, he began to wander the world, seeking a way to relieve suffering. Over a period of six years he amassed a group of five followers and practiced a variety of religions with different teachers. Though he studied and meditated in many forms, he was unable to find the true answer to his quest. It was then he determined to follow a more severe path, fasting entirely without food or water and enduring intense amount of pain at the same time. He was certain that this must be the way to full enlightenment and understanding.

After some time, he determined that this also was not the answer he sought and accepted a bowl of rice from a young girl he met during his travels. Upon eating and drinking as well as finally bathing in the river he determined that there had to be another way to achieve enlightenment than to pursue self-punishment. Though his followers deserted him, Siddhartha determined that there must be no extremism if one was to accomplish the goals he had for himself. The path he then forged, one of balance between pleasure and suffering, was named the 'Middle Way' and is still the way of Buddhists to this day.

Siddhartha determined that he would meditate instead

and that, before he rose again, the answer would come to him. It took several days of deep meditation, of looking inside himself, of clearing his mind, of reviewing his life and his past lives, before he found the beautiful state of enlightenment that he had sought. Fighting away the demons which attempted to claim his perfect state, he began to truly see and experience that which he had sought. He could finally understand suffering and had reached enlightenment for himself. It was in that moment he became Buddha.

His first sermon was over 100 miles away, where he found the five individuals with whom he had traveled previously. Though he had initially been uncertain about preaching at all, his first sermon, Setting in Motion the Wheel of the Dharma, allowed him to draw in followers who also wanted to reach the level of enlightenment that he was able to achieve. He outlined to them the Four Noble Truths and the Eightfold Path which will be discussed throughout later sections of this book and his followers created a community of monks known as Sangha to also seek the higher truth that Buddha had achieved. There were no barriers for those who wished to join Sangha and all, despite their race, class, sex or background, were allowed to join in the search for fulfillment.

Buddha continued to preach his sermons and his path to enlightenment until his passing at the age of 80. He became a beacon of hope for many, leading them down the path to fulfillment in their lives and to peace and happiness as well. Through his teachings, known as the Dharma, he was able to draw many more to Buddhism, throughout his own country and beyond as his teachings began to morph throughout the world.

Chapter 3: The Teachings of Buddhism

Throughout his life and his own enlightenment Buddha came to recognize Three Universal Truths, Four Noble Truths and the Noble Eightfold Path. Each of these can be used together to help anyone interested in improving their life. In this chapter we will talk about each of them and throughout the next chapters we'll help you understand more about how to apply each of them specifically to different aspects of your own life.

The Three Universal Truths
Nothing is Lost in the Universe

Buddha came to understand that everything that exists in the universe, from the smallest insect to the largest elephant is there for a purpose. Each creature, each plant is precious to the existence of life as we know it.

When a tree dies it decomposes into soil that is used by new trees. When that tree grows it produces the oxygen necessary for life. Because of oxygen, humans are capable of life. This basic tenant led to an understanding of the Buddha and his followers to never kill an animal.

Everything Changes

Life continues to grow. Throughout existence everything in life will continue to change and adapt. And not only does life continue to evolve but it is sometimes positive and sometimes negative. As things continue to advance and change life will never cease. As evidenced by the death and extinction of the dinosaurs, and the continuation of life to the present day, nothing ever truly ends and life will continue to go on.

Law of Cause and Effect

Finally, the Buddha determined that changes will continue to occur because of cause and effect. This idea is considered as karma and it states that everything will occur in a way that is representative of our own actions. When someone commits an action they are at risk of a reaction to occur as well. Though these reactions may be positive (as by someone committing a positive action) they may also be negative. Karma encourages those who follow Buddhism to continue to behave in a positive way at all times.

The Four Noble Truths
Suffering is Common to All

The Buddha emphasizes that suffering will occur and that it is impossible to avoid suffering entirely. As a result, it is important to understand what suffering is. In many situations such as sickness, old age, death or even birth anyone will feel suffering. In other situations however, such as being away from someone that they like and not getting the things that they want in life, many people will go through a period of suffering. And Buddha emphasized that suffering will occur and happiness cannot last forever.

We Are the Cause of Our Suffering

Because so many people live in ignorance and greed they do not live their lives in a way that can improve their karma. They end up with a large amount of bad karma and end up experiencing a lot more suffering. Because they act in a way that is not appropriate, always wanting more, they are incapable of ever achieving true peace and nirvana. This can come from being spoiled and from reaching too much for additional possessions rather than being happy with what one has.

Stop Doing What Causes Suffering

In order to cease the suffering that you are going through you need to give up greed and ignorance (the worst aspects of suffering). For a Buddhist the cessation of these emotions and feelings is called Nirvana. Achieving nirvana will allow for joy and everlasting peace but it is only possible if you are able to stop allowing greed to envelop your life and you are capable of divesting yourself of all desires as well.

Everyone Can Be Enlightened

Finally, anyone can achieve enlightenment. All it takes is following the Middle Way, the Noble Eightfold Path. If you follow this path and you continue to observe all of its teachings you will be capable of living an enlightened life in the same way as the Buddha was able to do. For all of his followers this path was the true way to achieve everything that they have been able to achieve and it is believed to be the best way for anyone else to achieve these same accomplishments as well. Following this path will end suffering.

The Noble Eightfold Path

Right View

In order to achieve spiritual enlightenment and to truly achieve everything that is capable of making you stronger and more fulfilled you must seek to view the world in the proper way. This requires you to look at the world with wisdom and compassion which is the way of the Buddha.

Right Thought

Thinking in a positive and clear way is essential to being able to achieve enlightenment. The Buddha teaches that we are the things that we think and therefore it is crucial that we think properly. By thinking kindly we are able to develop our character properly.

Right Speech

Speaking in the best way possible, speaking in a positive, kind and helpful manner, is the best way to gain the admiration of others. Though admiration is not necessary for full achievement of enlightenment, traits that go along with it such as respect and trust most definitely are.

Right Conduct

To achieve enlightenment it is also imperative that we carry ourselves in an appropriate way. This requires us to behave in the way that is best for the world and not just the way that is best for ourselves. We must also make sure to act in the way that we require others to act.

Right Livelihood

Working is a difficult aspect of Buddhism and of life in general. Because we must all find a way to make a living, it is crucial that we continue to uphold the teachings of Buddha even in our work. According to the Buddha we must do our best to achieve a living through a method that does not bring harm to anyone or anything or cause others to feel unhappy.

Right Effort

In doing the best that we possibly can at all times it is possible achieve much more. This means putting all of our effort forth to achieve what we should be working towards. It means not spending time in ways that are harmful and instead, spending our time in doing our very best in everything that we attempt or accomplish.

Right Mindfulness

Before we think, speak or do anything it is important

that we keep in our minds the proper ways of thinking and acting. We must be careful to consider all thoughts and actions before they are committed as, once done, these things are not simple to undo.

Right Concentration

Focus is crucial to success in any endeavor and most especially in this because it allows for the best ability possible to be put forward. Anyone who strives to complete a task must likewise strive to do it well.

In order to use each of these in the best way possible, anyone striving to follow Buddhism and achieve enlightenment must likewise consider the Three Jewels; the three different aspects of Buddhism which will allow them to follow the true path. These Three Jewels are extremely important and include The Buddha himself as the guide to the path, the Dharma (also the Eightfold Path) as the path to follow, and the Sangha as the teachers to lead you on your way.

The Five Precepts

Also included in Buddhism, much in the way they are included in Christianity, are five precepts or 'rules' not to break. Created directly by the Buddha, these instructions for life are crucial to anyone who wishes to achieve enlightenment because breaking them will cause the path to become muddied and potentially impassable as well. This makes it important to understand each aspect and why each aspect is so important to the following of the Buddha and his path.

Do Not Kill

The Buddhist teachings state that to kill one creature (any type of creature) is to bring about the death of oneself. A true Buddhist must have a love and caring for all creatures and must wish them to be free from any type of harm at all times. This goes for any creature from the soil to insects all the way to the largest creatures known to mankind. As such, Buddhists are generally expected to be vegetarian, so as to avoid injuring or killing any animals for their own pleasure or wellbeing.

Do Not Steal

Taking from someone else is showing a disregard for that other person. We must instead seek to provide for others rather than taking from them. In order to provide for others properly we must be sure not to take from them but to give whatever we can and whatever we believe we are able. This involves sharing what is available on our table no matter who with.

Do Not Commit Sexual Misconduct

Buddha believed that behaving in a proper way was the best way to show respect for our own body as well as for our parents who gave us life and the presence of that body. By behaving in a pure and virtuous way it is possible to improve the world in which we live and likewise to improve our own family and our own livelihood at the same time. This requires showing respect for all we come into contact with as well as ourselves.

Do Not Lie

To lie is to take away from the self and from those around you as well. By being honest, avoiding gossip and avoiding idle or harsh speech, it is possible for the world to fall into peace. By talking it is also possible to avoid misunderstanding and to therefore avoid anger.

Do Not Use Intoxicants

Intoxicating substances will only dull the mind and the senses. They will cause quarrel with family and friends and they further cause illness and weakness. As a result, the Buddha believes that there is no place for any type of intoxicants within his teachings. Instead, the body should remain healthy and pure and the mind must be kept clear so it is possible to achieve not only happiness but cleanliness as well. This will provide for enlightenment and for an easier way down the path toward that true enlightenment that the Buddha has promised......

Made in the USA
Middletown, DE
16 February 2018